INTERMEDIATE

SCAT

Grades 4-5

Larchmont Academics

LarchmontAcademics.com

To request permissions or inquire about buying this title in bulk, contact the publisher.

ISBN: 9798858199113

First paperback edition August 2022.

The School and College Ability Test (SCAT) is owned and operated by The Johns Hopkins Center for Talented Youth, which was not involved in the production of, and does not endorse, sponsor, or certify this product.

Published in the USA

Larchmont Academics
Los Angeles, CA

LarchmontAcademics.com

Table of Contents

PREPARING FOR THE TEST...**4**

    WHAT TO EXPECT ON THE SCAT 5

    STRATEGIES FOR THE VERBAL SECTION 6

    STRATEGIES FOR THE QUANTITATIVE SECTION..8

    TIMING STRATEGIES 10

PRACTICE TEST #1 ....**11**

    VERBAL TEST #1 12

    VERBAL TEST #1 – ANSWERS 23

    VERBAL TEST #1 – EXPLANATIONS 24

    QUANTITATIVE REASONING TEST #1 30

    QUANTITATIVE TEST #1 – ANSWERS 49

    QUANTITATIVE TEST #1 - EXPLANATIONS 50

PRACTICE TEST #2 ....**64**

    VERBAL TEST #2 65

    VERBAL TEST #2 – ANSWERS 76

    VERBAL TEST #2 – EXPLANATIONS 77

    QUANTITATIVE REASONING TEST #2 83

    QUANTITATIVE TEST #2 – ANSWERS 102

    QUANTITATIVE TEST #2 - EXPLANATIONS 103

PRACTICE TEST #3 ....**118**

    VERBAL TEST #3 119

    VERBAL TEST #3 – ANSWERS 130

    VERBAL TEST #3 – EXPLANATIONS 131

    QUANTITATIVE REASONING TEST #3 137

    QUANTITATIVE TEST #3 – ANSWERS 156

    QUANTITATIVE TEST #3 - EXPLANATIONS 157

SCAT SCORING **172**

    HOW SCORING WORKS 173

    ESTIMATING YOUR SCORES 174

Preparing for the Test

What to Expect on the SCAT

The SCAT has two sections: Verbal and Quantitative. This book will prepare you for both sections.

Each section is 22 minutes long and contains 55 questions.

Verbal Section
This section tests your understanding of meaning through word analogies. The goal is to determine the relationship between the word pairs. You then must find another word pair with a similar relationship.

Example:

1. good : great
    a. tremendous : amazing
    b. bad : terrible
    c. pretty : ugly
    d. nice : proud

Answer: B
Good is a lower degree of *great*. *Bad* is a lower degree of *terrible*.

Quantitative Section
This section tests your mathematical reasoning skills. The goal is to determine which value is greater or if both values are equal. Many of the questions do not require computation. Instead, the goal is to determine the answer through reasoning.

Example:

Column A	Column B
5 x 4 x 3 x 0	1 x 4 x 2

Answer: Column A is greater.
Column A is being multiplied by 0. Any number being multiplied by 0 will be 0. Column B will be larger than 0.

Strategies for the Verbal Section

Goal

Your goal is to determine the relationship between the word pair and then find a pair with a similar relationship.

1. pear : fruit
    a. cactus : fern
    b. dog : animal
    c. drink : food
    d. house : apartment

Connecting the Words

Create a simple sentence that shows the connection between the two words.

Example:

pear : fruit → A pear **is a type of** fruit.

Avoid simply saying "A pear is a fruit" because it is not specific enough.

Check the Answer Choices

Check the answer choices using your sentence.

    X Cactus is a type of fern
    ✓ dog is a type of animal
    X drink is a type of food
    X house is a type of apartment

Answer : B – A dog is a type of animal.

Common Relationships

Look for these common relationships.

____ is the same as ____

____ is the opposite of ____

____ is a type of ____

____ is a higher/lesser degree of ____

____ is the function of ____

____ is a tool for ____

____ is a person who ____

Strategies for the Quantitative Section

Goal

Your goal is to compare the value of Column A with the value of Column B.

1.

Column A	Column B
12 + 14 + 45 + 4	13 + 15 + 25 + 8

You will choose from three answer choices:
- A) Column A is greater
- B) Column B is greater
- C) Columns A and B are equal

Compare, don't <u>always</u> solve!

Often, you will not need to solve both column A and B to find the answer, instead, compare both sides.

Column A	Column B
12 + 14 + 45 + 4	13 + 15 + 25 + 8
45 is **twenty** higher than 25	13 is **one** higher than 12
	15 is **one** higher than 14
	8 is **four** higher than 8

Column A is greater because the difference of twenty in Column A is much higher than the differences in Column B

Be ready for common tricky question types!

Here are some common rules to know and be ready for!

Order of Operations – This is the order you solve ALL math problems in
1. **P**arenthesis and grouping symbols,
2. **E**xponents,
3. **M**ultiplication and **D**ivision from left to right,
4. **A**ddition and **S**ubtraction from left to right.

Factors

GCF (greatest common factor) – the highest number that goes into both numbers

LCM (lowest common multiple) – the lowest number both can be multiplied to become.

Prime numbers – numbers that can't be divided by anything except 1 and themselves. It is helpful to know this list: 2, 3, 5, 7, 11, 13, 17, 19, 23, 29, 31

Geometry

Angle Sums – The angles inside any four-sided figure add up to 360°, the angles inside any triangle add up to 180°

Area of a Triangle – The area of a triangle is ½(base x height)

Percentages

Breaking numbers down - To find 10% of any number, divide by 10. You can then use that number to find other percentages. For example, if you double it, you have 20%!

Flipped Percentages- 15% of 28 is the same as 28% of 15. This will work with all numbers!

Unit Comparisons

1000 millimeters = 1 meter
100 centimeters = 1 meter
1000 meters = 1 kilometer

12 inches = 1 foot
1 yard = 3 feet

Look at the answer explanations to learn other tips and strategies!

Timing Strategies

Keep Track of Your Timing

You only have 24 seconds per question. Some questions will take much less time than this and others will take much more. Instead of watching the clock at every question, check the clock after 10 questions. If you have 18 minutes to go or more, you are at a good pace. If not, work on moving at a faster pace. The best thing to do to work on your timing is to practice.

Every 4 minutes, you should be 10 questions further along.

Know when to guess and move on!

Unlike in school, you do not need to show work and be absolutely sure of your answer. Instead, the goal is to reason and make an assessment based on the information given. So, if you don't know something, take your best guess based on what you do know.

Practice Test #1

Verbal Test #1

55 Questions – 22 Minutes

1. abandon : forgo

    A) essential : personal

    B) mandatory : required

    C) elective : needed

    D) hopeful : positive

2. legendary : unimportant

    A) ignorant : gullible

    B) favorite : best

    C) amazing : incredible

    D) naive : experienced

3. root : leaf

    A) water : dirt

    B) sand : gravel

    C) foundation : roof

    D) cheese : sauce

4. emperor : ruler

    A) professor : teacher

    B) senator : monarch

    C) president : general

    D) pharaoh: friend

5. competent : proficient

    A) furtive : calm

    B) bewilder : astound

    C) anger : thankfulness

    D) evil : good

6. initiate : conclude

   A) steps : method

   B) purpose : goal

   C) similarity : difference

   D) angry : cheerful

7. drill : carpentry

   A) plow : farming

   B) hammer : saw

   C) blender : stove

   D) lighter : vacuum

8. cleaning : soap

   A) fiction : fact

   B) communication : phone

   C) sleeping : studying

   D) finish : commence

9. Undetermined : indefinite

   A) pretend : non-fiction

   B) desirable : unnecessary

   C) fallow : lush

   D) boycott : refuse

10. overjoyed : happy

    A) angry : playful

    B) depressed : sad

    C) ignoring : flirting

    D) fickle : decisive

11. toxic : harmless

    A) genuine : fake

    B) affiliated : related

    C) citizen : resident

    D) alien : foreign

12. welder : welds

    A) player : injures

    B) printer : printers

    C) fabricator : disassembles

    D) chef : cooks

13. octopus : tentacles

    A) fish : bird

    B) icicle : flame

    C) pig : hooves

    D) float : dive

14. famished : starved

    A) wandering : focused

    B) feeble : hearty

    C) energized : fatigued

    D) pristine : clean

15. observe : ignore

    A) create : design

    B) protect : defend

    C) emphasize : understate

    D) deflate : unhinge

16. fisherman : fishes

    A) person : human

    B) janitor : cleans

    C) handyman : hands

    D) fireman : delineates

17. Petal : flower

    A) fin : wing

    B) stick : straw

    C) sticker : syrup

    D) scale : fish

18. firm : unchangeable

    A) sickly : underling

    B) final : rage

    C) discouraged : hopeless

    D) fiesta : ire

19. button : snap

    A) pin : pine

    B) clasp : zipper

    C) couple : single

    D) fiasco : attire

20. allocate : withhold

    A) devastate : construct

    B) bind : tighten

    C) whimsical : flipper

    D) foldable : flighty

21. punctual : prompt

    A) fiery : watery

    B) complete : ended

    C) spotless : fastidious

    D) devious : sneaky

22. lever : pulley

    A) nail : taller

    B) spoon : eraser

    C) waffles : pancakes

    D) paint : bow

23. abruptly : suddenly

    A) consecutive : chronological

    B) aging : expansive

    C) flagrant : cascading

    D) tirade : diminutive

24. atmosphere : gases

    A) spherical : conical

    B) habitual : phonics

    C) hydrosphere : waters

    D) hydrophobia : stratosphere

25. listen : ignore

    A) witness : report

    B) diagram : explain

    C) graph : plot

    D) acquire : disperse

26. tango : dance

    A) nomad : station

    B) photography : art

    C) fantastic : ancient

    D) science : math

27. tired : lethargic

    A) condensation : baseline

    B) acidic : dehumidify

    C) energetic : hyperactive

    D) discard : file

28. interpret : decode

    A) recreation : travail

    B) filament : traffic

    C) hide : disguise

    D) wails : trails

29. spring : desert

    A) tundra : jungle

    B) stream : wilderness

    C) path : road

    D) cycle : division

30. monitor : supervise

    A) flash : thunder

    B) distance : idolize

    C) liturgy : momentary

    D) procrastinate : delay

31. handle : shovel

    A) structure : spike

    B) angle : turn

    C) mallet : hammer

    D) string : kite

32. accountant : money

    A) cashier : marketer

    B) psychologist : arborist

    C) doctor : kitchens

    D) mechanic : machines

33. car : metal

    A) pavement : sidewalk

    B) skin : hair

    C) statue : stone

    D) laptop : tablet

34. aggressive : cooperative

    A) filter : flood

    B) splatter : scan

    C) abundant : meager

    D) wither : shrivel

35. pine : oak

    A) deer : wolves

    B) popcorn : hay

    C) react : sabotage

    D) mitigate : engage

36. poised : confident

    A) undeserved : participant

    B) weary : loathsome

    C) sound : catapult

    D) awestruck : astonished

37. parallelogram : four

    A) edible : orange

    B) hexagon : six

    C) serendipitous : encounter

    D) triangle : five

38. radiologist : x-rays

    A) miner : radio

    B) backhoe : dentist

    C) habit : attitude

    D) navigator : maps

39. industrious : unproductive

    A) concur : disagree

    B) completely : totally

    C) abased : abashed

    D) private : confidential

40. planet : galaxy

    A) shapes : bees

    B) cell : body

    C) mats : shelves

    D) photography : bushes

41. city : town

    A) sanctuary : war

    B) refuge : solace

    C) stadium : auditorium.

    D) creek : park

42. eligible : qualified

    A) awaited : forthcoming

    B) bold : terrified

    C) futuristic : concentric

    D) flavorful : enveloped

43. pie : graph

    A) dog : bark

    B) octagon : polygon

    C) hippopotamus : giraffe.

    D) stuffed : filling

44. mitigate : alleviate

    A) narrate : explain

    B) father : mother

    C) pander : wonder

    D) dyed : frosting

45. glasses : eyes

    A) shoulders : strong

    B) hand : glove

    C) rancher : weeds

    D) braces : teeth

46. abnormal : common

    A) endure : escape

    B) hide : follow

    C) incorporate : combine

    D) task : meditate

47. hoe : weeding

    A) rake : shovel

    B) scraping : cutting

    C) ladder : climbing

    D) winter : spring

48. acres : land

    A) cubes : cubits

    B) inches : length

    C) dollars : wallet

    D) thunder : lightening

49. innocent : guiltless

    A) inevitable : unavoidable

    B) happenstance : possibility

    C) buttress : arch

    D) fragrant : odious

50. shame : compliment

    A) fountain : statue

    B) comforting : hometown

    C) hill : well

    D) irritating : soothing

51. team : players

    A) car : tires

    B) troop : soldiers

    C) secretary : noteworthy

    D) foul : feet

52. difficult : complex

    A) fluent : fealty

    B) compliant : encroaching

    C) boastful : arrogant

    D) simplistic : harrowing

53. gentle : vicious

    A) avoidance : holiness

    B) unscathed : harmed

    C) limited : lowly

    D) dream : door

54. ride : bike

    A) sign : contract

    B) taxi : truck

    C) litigate : fantasize

    D) memorial : obituary

55. treaty : agreement

    A) feasting : military

    B) boating : triumph

    C) punishment : wrongdoing

    D) drainage : water

Verbal Test #1 – Answers

1. B	20. A	39. A
2. D	21. D	40. B
3. C	22. C	41. C
4. A	23. A	42. A
5. B	24. C	43. B
6. D	25. D	44. A
7. A	26. B	45. D
8. B	27. C	46. A
9. D	28. C	47. C
10. B	29. B	48. B
11. A	30. D	49. A
12. D	31. D	50. D
13. C	32. D	51. B
14. D	33. C	52. C
15. C	34. C	53. B
16. B	35. A	54. A
17. D	36. D	55. C
18. C	37. B	
19. B	38. D	

Verbal Test #1 – Explanations

1. Answer: B
   Abandon **is the same as** forgo.
   Mandatory **is the same as** required.

2. Answer: D
   Legendary **is the opposite of** unimportant.
   Naïve **is the opposite of** experienced.

3. Answer: C
   A root **supports** a leaf.
   A foundation **supports** a roof

4. Answer: A
   An emperor **is a type** of ruler.
   A professor **is a type** of teacher.

5. Answer: B
   Competent **is the same as** proficient.
   Bewilder **is the same as** astound.

6. Answer: D
   Initiate **is the opposite of** terminate.
   Angry **is the opposite of** cheerful.

7. Answer: A
   A drill **is a tool for** carpentry.
   A plow **is a tool for** farming.

8. Answer: B
   Cleaning **is the function of** soap.
   Communication **is the function of** a phone.

9. Answer: D
   Undetermined **is the same as** indefinite.
   Boycott **is the same as** refuse.

10. Answer: B
    Overjoyed **is a higher degree of** happy.
    Depressed **is a higher degree of** sad.

11. Answer: A

Toxic **is the opposite of** harmless.

Genuine **is the opposite of** fake.

12. Answer: D

A welder **is a person who** welds.

A chef **is a person who** cooks.

13. Answer: C

An octopus **has** tentacles.

A pig **has** hooves.

14. Answer: D

Famished **means** starved.

Pristine **means** clean.

15. Answer: C

Observe **is the opposite of** ignore.

Emphasize **is the opposite of** understate.

16. Answer: B

A fisherman **is a person who** fishes.

A janitor a **is a person who** cleans.

17. Answer: D

A petal **is a part of** a flower.

A scale **is a part of** a fish.

18. Answer: C

Firm **is a lesser degree of** unchangeable.

Disappointed **is a lesser degree of** hopeless.

19. Answer: B

A button and a snap are **both types of** fasteners.

A clasp and a zipper are **both types of** closures.

20. Answer: A

Allocate **is the opposite of** withhold.

Devastate **is the opposite of** construct.

21. Answer: D

Punctual **is the same as** prompt.

Devious **is the same as** sneaky.

22. Answer: C

A lever and a pulley **are both types of** simple machines.

Waffles and pancakes **are both types of** breakfast breads.

23. Answer: A

Abruptly **is the same as** suddenly.

Consecutive **is the same as** chronological.

24. Answer: C

The atmosphere **consists of** gases.

The hydrosphere **consists of** waters.

25. Answer: D

Listen **is the opposite of** ignore.

Acquire **is the opposite of** disperse.

26. Answer: B

Tango **is a type of** dance.

Photography **is a type of** art.

27. Answer: C

Tired **is a lesser form of** lethargic.

Energetic **is a lesser form of** hyperactive.

28. Answer: C

Interpret **is the same as** decode.

Hide **is the same as** disguise.

29. Answer: B

A spring **functions as a water source** in the desert.

A stream **functions as a water source** in the wilderness.

30. Answer: D

Monitor **is the same as** supervise.

Procrastinate **is the same as** delay.

31. Answer: D

A handle **is used to hold** a shovel.

A string **is used to hold** a kite.

32. Answer: D
    An accountant **works with** money.
    A mechanic **works with** machines.

33. Answer: C
    A car **is made of** metal
    A statue **is made of** stone.

34. Answer: C
    Aggressive **is the opposite of** cooperative.
    Abundant **is the opposite of** meager.

35. Answer: A
    Pine and oak **are both types of** trees.
    Deer and wolves **are both types of** mammals.

36. Answer: D
    Poised **is the same as** confident.
    Awestruck **is the same as** astonished.

37. Answer: B
    A parallelogram **has** four **sides.**
    A hexagon **has** six **sides.**

38. Answer: D
    A radiologist **analyzes** x-rays.
    A navigator **analyzes** maps.

39. Answer: A
    Industrious **is the opposite of** unproductive.
    Concur **is the opposite of** disagree.

40. Answer: B
    A planet **is a part of** a galaxy.
    A cell **is a part of** a body.

41. Answer: C
    A city **is a higher degree of gathering** than a town.
    A stadium **is a higher degree of gathering** than an auditorium.

42. Answer: A
    Eligible **is the same as** qualified.
    Awaited **is the same as** forthcoming.

43. Answer: B

Pie **is a type of** graph.

Octagon **is a type of** polygon.

44. Answer: A

Mitigate **is the same as** alleviate.

Narrate **is the same as** explain.

45. Answer: D

Glasses **help** eyes.

Braces **help** teeth.

46. Answer: A

Abnormal **is the opposite of** common.

Endure **is the opposite of** escape.

47. Answers: C

A hoe **is a tool used for** weeding.

A ladder **is a tool used for** climbing.

48. Answers: B

Acres **are often used to measure** land.

Inches **are often used to measure** televisions.

49. Answers: A

Innocent **is the same as** guiltless.

Inevitable **is the same as** unavoidable.

50. Answers: D

Shame **is the opposite of** compliment.

Irritating **is the opposite of** soothing.

51. Answers: B

A team **is composed of many** players.

A troop **is composed of many** soldiers.

52. Answers: C

Difficult **is the same as** complex.

Boastful **is the same as** arrogant.

53. Answers: B

Gentle **is the opposite of** vicious.

Unscathed **is the opposite of** harmed.

54. Answers: A

Sign **is what one does with a** contract.
Ride **is what one does with a** bike.

55. Answers: C

A treaty **is the result of an** agreement.
A punishment **is the result of a** wrongdoing.

Quantitative Reasoning Test #1

55 Questions – 22 Minutes

1.

Column A	Column B
$3(4x + 20)$	$12x + 60$

A) Column A is greater.

B) Column B is greater.

C) Columns A and B are equal.

D) The relationship cannot be determined with the information given.

2.

Column A	Column B
The sum of the even numbers from 1-8	The sum of the odd numbers from 1-8

A) Column A is greater.

B) Column B is greater.

C) Columns A and B are equal.

D) The relationship cannot be determined with the information given.

3.

Column A	Column B
The mean of 4, 6, 8, 10	The range of 3, 5, 8, 10

A) Column A is greater.

B) Column B is greater.

C) Columns A and B are equal.

D) The relationship cannot be determined with the information given.

4.

Column A	Column B
$4 \times 5 - (10 \div 2 + 3)$	$4 \times 5 - 10 \div (2 + 3)$

A) Column A is greater.

B) Column B is greater.

C) Columns A and B are equal.

D) The relationship cannot be determined with the information given.

5.

Column A	Column B
$\dfrac{7}{4} \times \dfrac{4}{3}$	$\dfrac{2}{5} \times \dfrac{5}{3}$

A) Column A is greater.

B) Column B is greater.

C) Columns A and B are equal.

D) The relationship cannot be determined with the information given.

6.

Column A	Column B
The perimeter of a rectangle with a height of 3 and a length of 4	The area of a rectangle with a height of 3 and a length of 4

A) Column A is greater.

B) Column B is greater.

C) Columns A and B are equal.

D) The relationship cannot be determined with the information given.

7.

Column A	Column B
50% of 250	15% of 300

A) Column A is greater.

B) Column B is greater.

C) Columns A and B are equal.

D) The relationship cannot be determined with the information given.

8.

Column A	Column B
The GCF of 12 and 15	The GCF of 9 and 18

A) Column A is greater.

B) Column B is greater.

C) Columns A and B are equal.

D) The relationship cannot be determined with the information given.

9.

Column A	Column B
The area of a triangle with a base of 10 and a height of 4	The area of a square with a side length of 5

A) Column A is greater.

B) Column B is greater.

C) Columns A and B are equal.

D) The relationship cannot be determined with the information given.

10.
There are 7 ducks, 4 frogs, and 2 swans in a pond.

Column A	Column B
The ratio of frogs to swans	The ratio of frogs to ducks

A) Column A is greater.

B) Column B is greater.

C) Columns A and B are equal.

D) The relationship cannot be determined with the information given.

11.

Column A	Column B
The smallest prime number between 12 and 30	17

A) Column A is greater.

B) Column B is greater.

C) Columns A and B are equal.

D) The relationship cannot be determined with the information given.

12.

Column A	Column B
24% of 50	50% of 24

A) Column A is greater.

B) Column B is greater.

C) Columns A and B are equal.

D) The relationship cannot be determined with the information given.

13.

$x > 1$

Column A	Column B
$3x$	$\dfrac{x}{3}$

A) Column A is greater.

B) Column B is greater.

C) Columns A and B are equal.

D) The relationship cannot be determined with the information given.

14.

Column A	Column B
$5^3 \times 5^2$	5^6

A) Column A is greater.

B) Column B is greater.

C) Columns A and B are equal.

D) The relationship cannot be determined with the information given.

15.

Column A	Column B
$\dfrac{9}{36}$	$\dfrac{7}{28}$

A) Column A is greater.

B) Column B is greater.

C) Columns A and B are equal.

D) The relationship cannot be determined with the information given.

16.

Column A	Column B
LCM of (5, 3)	GCF of (30, 15)

A) Column A is greater.

B) Column B is greater.

C) Columns A and B are equal.

D) The relationship cannot be determined with the information given.

17. A pack of pencils costs $1.50, a pack of pens cost $3, and a notebook costs $6.

Column A	Column B
The cost of two packs of pencils and a notebook	The cost of three packs of pens

A) Column A is greater.

B) Column B is greater.

C) Columns A and B are equal.

D) The relationship cannot be determined with the information given.

18.

Column A	Column B
$3(4 + 2) - 4^2$	$3 + (4 + 2) - 4^2$

A) Column A is greater.

B) Column B is greater.

C) Columns A and B are equal.

D) The relationship cannot be determined with the information given.

19.

Column A	Column B
$\dfrac{3}{4} \times \dfrac{1}{2}$	$\dfrac{3}{4} \div \dfrac{1}{4}$

A) Column A is greater.

B) Column B is greater.

C) Columns A and B are equal.

D) The relationship cannot be determined with the information given.

20.

Column A	Column B
The next number in the series 14, 17, 20 , ___	The next number in the series 1, 3, 9, ___

A) Column A is greater.

B) Column B is greater.

C) Columns A and B are equal.

D) The relationship cannot be determined with the information given.

21.

Column A	Column B
$10^4 + 10$	10^5

A) Column A is greater.

B) Column B is greater.

C) Columns A and B are equal.

D) The relationship cannot be determined with the information given.

22.

Column A	Column B
0.4	0.4×0.2

A) Column A is greater.

B) Column B is greater.

C) Columns A and B are equal.

D) The relationship cannot be determined with the information given.

23.

Column A	Column B
0.01×90	10×0.09

A) Column A is greater.

B) Column B is greater.

C) Columns A and B are equal.

D) The relationship cannot be determined with the information given.

24.

Column A	Column B
The value of one quarter, one dime, and one nickel	The value of eight nickels

A) Column A is greater.

B) Column B is greater.

C) Columns A and B are equal.

D) The relationship cannot be determined with the information given.

25.

Column A	Column B
The number of days in a year	30×12

A) Column A is greater.

B) Column B is greater.

C) Columns A and B are equal.

D) The relationship cannot be determined with the information given.

26.

Column A	Column B
$4.526 + 3.01$	$5.021 + 2.34$

A) Column A is greater.

B) Column B is greater.

C) Columns A and B are equal.

D) The relationship cannot be determined with the information given.

27.

Column A	Column B
$\sqrt{64}$	$\dfrac{8^4}{8^3}$

A) Column A is greater.

B) Column B is greater.

C) Columns A and B are equal.

D) The relationship cannot be determined with the information given.

28.

Column A	Column B
The discount on an item that costs x and is 15% off	The discount on an item that costs y and is 25% off

A) Column A is greater.

B) Column B is greater.

C) Columns A and B are equal.

D) The relationship cannot be determined with the information given.

29.

Column A	Column B
$628 + 24 + 43 - 3$	$626 + 25 + 44 - 3$

A) Column A is greater.

B) Column B is greater.

C) Columns A and B are equal.

D) The relationship cannot be determined with the information given.

30.

Column A	Column B
$308 - 45 - 1^4$	$308 - 42 - 1$

A) Column A is greater.

B) Column B is greater.

C) Columns A and B are equal.

D) The relationship cannot be determined with the information given.

31.

Column A	Column B
$\dfrac{1}{4} \times 32$	$\sqrt{36}$

A) Column A is greater.

B) Column B is greater.

C) Columns A and B are equal.

D) The relationship cannot be determined with the information given.

32.

Column A	Column B
3^{24}	1^{88}

A) Column A is greater.

B) Column B is greater.

C) Columns A and B are equal.

D) The relationship cannot be determined with the information given.

33. Avery has 7 coins. The total value of her coins is 35 cents.

Column A	Column B
The number of pennies Avery has	The number of nickels Avery has

A) Column A is greater.

B) Column B is greater.

C) Columns A and B are equal.

D) The relationship cannot be determined with the information given.

34.

Column A	Column B
The perimeter of a hexagon with side lengths of 4	The perimeter of a pentagon with side lengths of 5

A) Column A is greater.

B) Column B is greater.

C) Columns A and B are equal.

D) The relationship cannot be determined with the information given.

35.

Column A	Column B
The amount Layla made per hour if she worked for four hours and made $48	The number of miles driven if a car drove at a rate of 30 miles per hour for half an hour

A) Column A is greater.

B) Column B is greater.

C) Columns A and B are equal.

D) The relationship cannot be determined with the information given.

36.

Column A	Column B
The measure of a right angle	The measure of the third angle in a triangle where the first angle is 60 degrees and second angle is 90 degrees

A) Column A is greater.

B) Column B is greater.

C) Columns A and B are equal.

D) The relationship cannot be determined with the information given.

37. $y = 4 - 5x$

Column A	Column B
The value of y if x is 10	The value of y if x is 11

A) Column A is greater.

B) Column B is greater.

C) Columns A and B are equal.

D) The relationship cannot be determined with the information given.

38. $a < b$

Column A	Column B
$4a$	$4b$

A) Column A is greater.

B) Column B is greater.

C) Columns A and B are equal.

D) The relationship cannot be determined with the information given.

39. Data set: 3, 3, 5, 7, 8, 8, 10, 12, 14

Column A	Column B
The median of the data set above	The range of the data set above

A) Column A is greater.

B) Column B is greater.

C) Columns A and B are equal.

D) The relationship cannot be determined with the information given.

40. Jaelyn shared her birthday cake with 5 friends. Jaelyn and each of her friends ate a slice that was 1/8 of the cake.

Column A	Column B
The amount of the cake left	$\dfrac{1}{4}$

A) Column A is greater.

B) Column B is greater.

C) Columns A and B are equal.

D) The relationship cannot be determined with the information given.

41.

Column A	Column B
$\sqrt{144}$	$\dfrac{1}{3}$ of 36

A) Column A is greater.

B) Column B is greater.

C) Columns A and B are equal.

D) The relationship cannot be determined with the information given.

42. Jordan had 135 baseball cards. He sold 3/5 of his cards to his friends.

Column A	Column B
The number of cards Jordan still has	The number of cards he sold

A) Column A is greater.

B) Column B is greater.

C) Columns A and B are equal.

D) The relationship cannot be determined with the information given.

43.

$$7z + 4 = 18$$

Column A	Column B
The value of z	7

A) Column A is greater.

B) Column B is greater.

C) Columns A and B are equal.

D) The relationship cannot be determined with the information given.

44.

Column A	Column B
$\frac{3}{4}$ of 60	$\frac{2}{3}$ of 90

A) Column A is greater.

B) Column B is greater.

C) Columns A and B are equal.

D) The relationship cannot be determined with the information given.

45.

Column A	Column B
The side length of a square with an area of 36	The width of a rectangle with an area of 20 and a height of 4

A) Column A is greater.

B) Column B is greater.

C) Columns A and B are equal.

D) The relationship cannot be determined with the information given.

46. $x > 2$

Column A	Column B
$\dfrac{9x + 7}{4}$	$\dfrac{9x - 7}{4}$

A) Column A is greater.

B) Column B is greater.

C) Columns A and B are equal.

D) The relationship cannot be determined with the information given.

47.

Column A	Column B
The LCM of 12, 15, and 20	The sum of 12, 15, and 20

A) Column A is greater.

B) Column B is greater.

C) Columns A and B are equal.

D) The relationship cannot be determined with the information given.

48. Jerimiah caught fewer fish than Anya. Anya caught more fish than Aiden. Ella caught more fish than Anya.

Column A	Column B
The number of fish Jerimiah caught	The number of fish Ella caught

A) Column A is greater.

B) Column B is greater.

C) Columns A and B are equal.

D) The relationship cannot be determined with the information given.

49. The number of students on the soccer team is 10 less than four times the number of students on the tennis team. There are x students on the tennis team.

Column A	Column B
$4x - 10$	The number of students on the soccer team

A) Column A is greater.

B) Column B is greater.

C) Columns A and B are equal.

D) The relationship cannot be determined with the information given.

50. A bag contains 5 red candies, 3 blue candies, and 4 green candies.

Column A	Column B
The probability of randomly selecting a blue candy or a green candy.	The probability of randomly selecting a red candy

A) Column A is greater.

B) Column B is greater.

C) Columns A and B are equal.

D) The relationship cannot be determined with the information given.

51. A wheel spins 24 times in 6 seconds.

Column A	Column B
The number of times the wheel spins in 2 seconds	$\sqrt{16}$

A) Column A is greater.

B) Column B is greater.

C) Columns A and B are equal.

D) The relationship cannot be determined with the information given.

52.

Column A	Column B
$\dfrac{4}{5} + \dfrac{2}{5}$	$\dfrac{3}{4} + \dfrac{3}{4}$

A) Column A is greater.

B) Column B is greater.

C) Columns A and B are equal.

D) The relationship cannot be determined with the information given.

53.

Column A	Column B
The number of hours between 10:30 am and 2:15 pm	4 hours and 15 minutes

A) Column A is greater.

B) Column B is greater.

C) Columns A and B are equal.

D) The relationship cannot be determined with the information given.

54.

Column A	Column B
The value of x if $-4 + 2x = 8$	The value of y if $3y - 4 = 2y$

A) Column A is greater.

B) Column B is greater.

C) Columns A and B are equal.

D) The relationship cannot be determined with the information given.

55.

Column A	Column B
12.45×10^4	1245×10^2

A) Column A is greater.

B) Column B is greater.

C) Columns A and B are equal.

D) The relationship cannot be determined with the information given.

Quantitative Test #1 – Answers

1. C	20. B	39. B
2. A	21. B	40. C
3. C	22. A	41. C
4. B	23. C	42. B
5. A	24. C	43. B
6. A	25. A	44. B
7. A	26. A	45. A
8. B	27. C	46. A
9. B	28. D	47. A
10. A	29. C	48. B
11. B	30. B	49. C
12. B	31. A	50. A
13. A	32. A	51. A
14. B	33. D	52. B
15. C	34. B	53. B
16. C	35. B	54. A
17. C	36. A	55. C
18. A	37. A	
19. B	38. B	

Quantitative Test #1 - Explanations

1. **C**

Column A	Column B
$3(4x + 20)$	$12x + 60$
$3(4x) + 3(20)$	
$12x + 60$	

2. **A**

Column A	Column B
The sum of the even numbers from 1-8	The sum of the odd numbers from 1-8
$2, 4, 6, 8$	$1, 3, 5, 7$
Each number is one higher than the number in its spot in column B. The sum will be higher.	

3. **C**

Column A	Column B
The mean of $4, 6, 8, 10$	The range of $3, 5, 8, 10$
$10 + 8 + 10 = 28$	$10 - 3 = 7$
$28 \div 4 = 7$	

4. **B**

Column A	Column B
$4 \times 5 - (10 \div 2 + 3)$	$4 \times 5 - 10 \div (2 + 3)$
$20 - (5 + 3)$	$20 - 10 \div 5$
$20 - 8$	$20 - 2$
12	18

5. **A**

Column A	Column B
$\dfrac{7}{4} \times \dfrac{4}{3}$	$\dfrac{2}{5} \times \dfrac{5}{3}$
$\dfrac{7}{1} \times \dfrac{1}{3} = \dfrac{7}{3}$	$\dfrac{2}{1} \times \dfrac{1}{3} = \dfrac{2}{3}$

6. **A**

Column A	Column B
The perimeter of a rectangle with a height of 3 and a length of 4	The area of a rectangle with a height of 3 and a length of 4
$3 + 3 + 4 + 4 = 14$	$3 \times 4 = 12$

7. **A**

Column A	Column B
50% of 250	15% of 300
125	10% = 30 5% = 15
	15% = 45
	OR without solving, reason that 15% of 300 will be much smaller than 125.

8. **B**

Column A	Column B
The GCF of 12 and 15	The GCF of 9 and 18
3	9

9. **B**

Column A	Column B
The area of a triangle with a base of 10 and a height of 4	The area of a square with a side length of 5
$\dfrac{b \times h}{2} = area\ of\ a\ triangle$	$5 \times 5 = 25$
$\dfrac{10 \times 4}{2} = 20$	

10. **A**

There are 7 ducks, 4 frogs, and 2 swans in a pond.

Column A	Column B
The ratio of frogs to swans	The ratio of frogs to ducks
4:2	4:7
To compare, think of it like a fraction. $\dfrac{4}{2} = 2$	$\dfrac{4}{7}$
	Less than 1

11. **B**

Column A	Column B
The smallest prime number between 12 and 30	17
13	

12. **C**

Column A	Column B
24% of 50	50% of 24
Fun trick - these will always be the same!	*Fun trick - these will always be the same!*

13. **A**

$x > 1$

Column A	Column B
$3x$	$\dfrac{x}{3}$
Multiply by 3. Ex: $3 \times 2 = 6$	Divide by 3. Ex: $\dfrac{2}{3}$

14. **B**

Column A	Column B
$5^3 \times 5^2$	5^6
$5 \times 5 \times 5 \times 5 \times 5$	$5 \times 5 \times 5 \times 5 \times 5 \times 5$

15. **C**

Column A	Column B
$\dfrac{9}{36}$	$\dfrac{7}{28}$
$\dfrac{9}{36} \rightarrow \dfrac{1}{4}$	$\dfrac{7}{28} \rightarrow \dfrac{1}{4}$

16. **C**

Column A	Column B
LCM of $(5, 3)$	GCF of $(30, 15)$
15	15

17. **C**

A pack of pencils costs $1.50, a pack of pens cost $3, and a notebook costs $6.

Column A	Column B
The cost of two packs of pencils and a notebook	The cost of three packs of pens
	$3 \times 3 = 9$
$1.50 + 1.50 + 6$	
$3 + 6 = 9$	

18. **A**

Column A	Column B
$3(4 + 2) - 4^2$	$3 + (4 + 2) - 4^2$
$3(6) - 16$	$3 + 6 - 16$
$18 - 16$	$9 - 16$
2	-7

19. **B**

Column A	Column B
$\dfrac{3}{4} \times \dfrac{1}{2}$	$\dfrac{3}{4} \div \dfrac{1}{4}$
$\dfrac{3}{4} \times \dfrac{1}{2} = \dfrac{3}{8}$	$\dfrac{3}{4} \times \dfrac{4}{1} = \dfrac{12}{4} = 3$

20. **B**

Column A	Column B
The next number in the series 14, 17, 20 , ___	The next number in the series 1, 3, 9 , ___
Add 3.	Multiply by 3.
23	27

21. **B**

Column A	Column B
$10^4 + 10$	10^5
$10 \times 10 \times 10 \times 10 + \mathbf{10}$	$10 \times 10 \times 10 \times 10 \times \mathbf{10}$
	Multiplying by 10 will increase it more than adding 10.

22. **A**

Column A	Column B
0.4	0.4×0.2
0.4	$4 \times 2 = 8.0$ Move the decimal 2 places to the left. 0.08

23. **C**

Column A	Column B
0.01×90	10×0.09
$0.01 \times 9 \times 10$	$10 \times 9 \times 0.01$

24. **C**

Column A	Column B
The value of one quarter, one dime, and one nickel	The value of eight nickels
	8×5
$25 + 10 + 5$ 40	40

25. **A**

Column A	Column B
The number of days in a year	30×12
365	360

26. **A**

Column A	Column B
$4.526 + 3.01$	$5.021 + 2.34$
$4.5 + 3$	$5 + 2.34$
7.5	7.34

27. **C**

Column A	Column B
$\sqrt{64}$	$\dfrac{8^4}{8^3}$
8	$\dfrac{8 \times 8 \times 8 \times 8}{8 \times 8 \times 8}$
	8

28. **D**

Column A	Column B
The discount on an item that costs x and is 15% off.	The discount on an item that costs y and is 25% off.
No information on the cost: Could be 1 dollar, Could be 1000 dollars	A different cost with no information: Could be 1 dollar, Could be 1000 dollars

29. **C**

Column A	Column B
$628 + 24 + 43 - 3$	$626 + 25 + 44 - 3$
2 higher, 1 lower, 1 lower, same	2 lower, 1 higher, 1 higher, same

30. **B**

Column A	Column B
$308 - 45 - 1^4$	$308 - 42 - 1$
$308 - 45 - 1$	$308 - 42 - 1$
Subtracting 3 more	

31. **A**

Column A	Column B
$\frac{1}{4} \times 32$	$\sqrt{36}$
$\frac{32}{4} = 8$	6

32. **A**

Column A	Column B
3^{24}	1^{88}
3 times itself 24 times	1

33. **D**

Avery has 7 coins. The total value of her coins is 35 cents.

Column A	Column B
The number of pennies Avery has	The number of nickels Avery has
Could have 7 nickels OR Could have 1 quarter, 1 nickel, and 5 pennies	Could have 7 nickels OR Could have 1 quarter, 1 nickel, and 5 pennies

34. **B**

Column A	Column B
The perimeter of a hexagon with side lengths of 4	The perimeter of a pentagon with side lengths of 5
$4 \times 6 = 24$	$5 \times 5 = 25$

35. **B**

Column A	Column B
The amount Layla made per hour if she worked for four hours and made $48	The number of miles driven if a car drove at a rate of 30 miles per hour for half an hour.
$48 \div 4 = 12$	1 hour = 30 miles Half an hour = 15 miles

36. **A**

Column A	Column B
The measure of a right angle	The measure of the third angle in a triangle where the first angle is 60 degrees and second angle is 90 degrees
90 degrees	Total measure of angles in a triangle = 180 degrees $180 - 60 - 90$ is less than 90

37. **A**

$y = 4 - 5x$

Column A	Column B
The value of y if x is 10	The value of y if x is 11
$y = 4 - 5(10)$ $y = 4 - 50$	$y = 4 - 5(11)$ $y = 4 - 55$ Subtracting more than Column A

38. **B**

$a < b$

Column A	Column B
$4a$	$4b$
4 times a lower number	4 times a higher number

39. **B**

Data set: 3, 3, 5, 7, 8, 8, 10, 12, 14

Column A	Column B
The median of the data set above	The range of the data set above
Middle number 3, 3, 5, 7, 8, 8, 10, 12, 14 8	$14 - 3 = 11$

40. **C**

Jaelyn shared her birthday cake with 5 friends. Jaelyn and each of her friends ate a slice that was 1/8 of the cake.

Column A	Column B
The amount of the cake left	$\dfrac{1}{4}$
$\dfrac{1}{8} \times 6 = \dfrac{6}{8} \ or \ \dfrac{3}{4}$ $\dfrac{1}{4}$ left	

41. **C**

Column A	Column B
$\sqrt{144}$	$\frac{1}{3}$ of 36
12	$\frac{36}{3} = 12$

42. **B**

Jordan had 135 baseball cards. He sold 3/5 of his cards to his friends.

Column A	Column B
The number of cards Jordan still has	The number of cards he sold
2/5	3/5

43. **B**

$7z + 4 = 18$

Column A	Column B
$7z + 4 = 18$	7
$7z = 14$	
$z = 2$	

44. **B**

Column A	Column B
$\frac{3}{4}$ of 60	$\frac{2}{3}$ of 90
$\frac{1}{4}$ of 60 = 15	$\frac{1}{3}$ of 90 = 30
$\frac{3}{4} = 45$	$\frac{2}{3} = 60$

45. **A**

Column A	Column B
The side length of a square with an area of 36	The width of a rectangle with an area of 20 and a height of 4
$\sqrt{36} = 6$	$4 \times width = 20$ $width = 5$

46. **A**

$x > 2$

Column A	Column B
$\dfrac{9x + 7}{4}$	$\dfrac{9x - 7}{4}$
$+7$	-7

47. **A**

Column A	Column B
The LCM of 12, 15, and 20	The sum of 12, 15, and 20
60	$27 + 20 = 47$

48. **B**

Jerimiah caught fewer fish than Anya. Anya caught more fish than Aiden. Ella caught more fish than Anya.

Column A	Column B
The number of fish Jerimiah caught	The number of fish Ella caught
Fewer than Anya	More than Anya

49. **C**

The number of students on the soccer team is 10 less than four times the number of students on the tennis team. There are x students on the tennis team.

Column A	Column B
$4x - 10$	The number of students on the soccer team
	Four times the number – 10 $4x - 10$

50. **A**

A bag contains 5 red candies, 3 blue candies, and 4 green candies.

Column A	Column B
The probability of randomly selecting a blue candy or a green candy 7/12	The probability of randomly selecting a red candy 5/12

51. **A**

A wheel spins 24 times in 6 seconds.

Column A	Column B
The number of times the wheel spins in 2 seconds 4 times in 1 second 8 times in 2 seconds	$\sqrt{16}$ 4

52. **B**

Column A	Column B
$\frac{4}{5} + \frac{2}{5}$ $\frac{4}{5} + \frac{2}{5} = \frac{6}{5}$	$\frac{3}{4} + \frac{3}{4}$ $\frac{3}{4} + \frac{3}{4} = \frac{6}{4}$

Given that numerators are the same, if the denominator is smaller, the fraction is bigger. A smaller denominator means the pieces of the pie are bigger.

53. **B**

Column A	Column B
The number of hours between 10:30 am and 2:15 pm	4 hours and 15 minutes
10:30 to 2:30 is 4 hours. Subtract 15 minutes to get to 2:15	
3 hours and 45 minutes	

54. **A**

Column A	Column B
The value of x if $-4 + 2x = 8$	The value of y if $3y - 4 = 2y$
$2x = 12$ $x = 6$	$3y - 4 = 2y$ $y = 4$

55. **C**

Column A	Column B
12.45×10^4	1245×10^2
124500	124500

Practice
Test #2

Verbal Test #2

55 Questions– 22 Minutes

---

1. intimidate : threaten

   A) finalize : navigate

   B) subtle : strong

   C) frequent : triumphant

   D) diminish : lessen

2. poverty : prosperity

   A) welcome : freedom

   B) success : failure

   C) weddings : hijinks

   D) powerful : wicked

3. blade : saw

   A) string : guitar

   B) tine : spoon

   C) line : hood

   D) fleece : pocket

4. cup : mug

   A) parameters : parallel

   B) shaded : perpendicular

   C) parallelogram : hexagon

   D) talented : suitable

5. independence : dependence

   A) subjective : objective

   B) size : frame

   C) blame : bliss

   D) shame : total

6. contributor : participant

    A) student : onlooker

    B) teacher : wisdom

    C) shopper : consumer

    D) plaintiff : tirades

7. car : carriage

    A) computer : typewriter

    B) farmer : fiddle

    C) bait : fish

    D) wheeled : triangular

8. peak : base

    A) cleaners : sanitize

    B) oils : wash

    C) cities : triads

    D) urban : rural

9. home : dwelling

    A) sugar : floating

    B) perimeter : border

    C) turning : timing

    D) tripped : dealt

10. scissors : shears

    A) plumb : level

    B) racket : rachet

    C) knife : saw

    D) grease : slime

11. waxing : waning

    A) Multiplying : dividing

    B) envelope : hold

    C) revenge : condemn

    D) pithy : pity

12. argument : feud

    A) tattered : friendly

    B) playground : water

    C) franchise : lightly

    D) pout : tantrum

13. income : compensation

    A) basket : box

    B) brim : hat

    C) card : cash

    D) bills : expenses

14. subtly : blatantly

    A) emotionally : mentally

    B) insufficiently : successfully

    C) mentally : thoughtfully

    D) spiritually : religiously

15. papaya : watermelon

    A) rainforest : swamp

    B) prissy : rickety

    C) vitamin : health

    D) frigid : freezer

16. balanced : unequal

    A) coating : waffling

    B) typical: eccentric

    C) overstate : handshake

    D) swiftly : psychedelic

17. accelerate : expedite

    A) unavoidable : purposeful

    B) chandelier : garage

    C) aspire : strive

    D) potable : habitable

18. archipelago : islands

    A) velum : fiberglass

    B) fulfillment : refrigeration

    C) creation : amazement

    D) constellation : stars

19. teaspoons : medicine

    A) centimeters : milk

    B) gallons : gasoline

    C) miles : feelings

    D) liters : sunshine

20. annihilate : exterminate

    A) disturb : agitate

    B) sinister : superior

    C) interior : exterior

    D) preposterous : extension

21. trumpet : brass

    A) drum : brass

    B) percussion : marching

    C) clarinet : woodwind

    D) band : chorus

22. spending : saving

    A) censoring : filtering

    B) borrowing : loaning

    C) disfunction : repurpose

    D) reflect : recycle

23. barrier : blockade

    A) boycott : reject

    B) tempt : attempt

    C) humongous : obnoxious

    D) undergo : imagine

24. hurricane : typhoon

    A) arid : dry

    B) smoky : clairvoyant

    C) cloudy : clear

    D) tangible : wispy

25. filthy : sterile

    A) float : filer

    B) presenter : teacher

    C) protector : defender

    D) disagree : compromise

26. emblem : symbol

    A) unchanged: transformed

    B) remarkable :   random

    C) conversation : discourse

    D) propaganda : predictability

27. ceremoniously : adverb

    A) but : preposition

    B) timid : adjective

    C) sofa : pronoun

    D) toward : conjunction

28. bird : nest

    A) tarantula : house

    B) beaver : dam

    C) creek : rain

    D) dolphins : echolocation

29. agriculture : farming

    A) disinfectant : spray

    B) irrigation : watering

    C) infuriate : interrogate

    D) firm : flexible

30. pentagon : polygon

    A) scatter plot : graph

    B) traveler : tortoise

    C) captain : ship

    D) chlorine : fluoride

31. import : export

    A) much : many

    B) filet : diced

    C) trident : survivor

    D) scarce : plentiful

32. frog : amphibian

    A) reptile : scaly

    B) owl : bird

    C) ostrich : raven

    D) pepper : spice

33. judicial : legislative

    A) executive : monetary

    B) cavalry : arms

    C) navy : army

    D) flight : presidential

34. lie : fabricate

    A) anger : infuriate

    B) hurt : heal

    C) mend : tear

    D) cost : change

35. enthrall : bore

    A) timeliness : penitence

    B) ponder : forget

    C) penniless : frugalness

    D) affiliate : transcontinental

36. plumbing : water

    A) pliers : cut

    B) battery : AAA

    C) wiring : electricity

    D) switch : light

37. paddle : kayak

    A) window : dingy

    B) sail : sailboat

    C) river : canoe

    D) journey : canal

38. condensation : evaporation

    A) soccer : karate

    B) comedy : tragedy

    C) microwave : braggart

    D) infant : homogenize

39. nomadic : migratory

    A) barter : trade

    B) deceitful : ingenious

    C) cynical : tolerable

    D) trampoline : buoyant

40. quadruple : four

    A) trial : triage

    B) quintuple : five

    C) tablet : troupe

    D) attractive : seven

41. traditional : classical

    A) bricks : logs

    B) detainee : restrain

    C) restrict : tradition

    D) sponsor : support

42. mono : one

    A) photo : graph

    B) able : can

    C) poly : many

    D) anti : for

43. coach : teacher

    A) daughter : covenant

    B) contract : obligated

    C) baker : chef

    D) automated : pledge

44. monsoon : rain

    A) cyclone : snowstorm

    B) sandstorm : tsunami

    C) earthquake : volcano

    D) tornado : wind

45. singer : songs

    A) comedian : jokes

    B) cartoon : adventure

    C) drama : documentary

    D) laughter : songs

46. desert : biome

    A) dinosaur : pterodactyl

    B) crimson : jaundiced

    C) lettuce : vegetable

    D) dreamscape : feverish

47. connotation : undertone

    A) negligent : inattentive

    B) occupational : promotional

    C) hazards : glacial

    D) fragmented : rivals

48. discern : misinterpret

    A) incandescent : neon

    B) fruitful : ineffective

    C) fluorescent : fixated

    D) patrol : soul

49. conjecture : assumption

    A) probability : likelihood

    B) compatibility : guesses

    C) handsome : flotsam

    D) antique : litigate

50. radius : diameter

    A) fungal : radial

    B) inch : acre

    C) whisperer : whistler

    D) pint : quart

51. spirit : spunk

    A) trick : blame

    B) train : fund

    C) ajar : unlatched

    D) trample : simplify

52. validate : deny

    A) pretend : fish

    B) astute : foolish

    C) pacify : determine

    D) mandate : intercept

53. rupture : fissure

    A) tempest : statistic

    B) concentration : stormy

    C) confusion : assumption

    D) greedy : avaricious

54. exclusion : acceptance

    A) lavish : destitute

    B) presentation : inclusion

    C) anteater : demonstration

    D) funeral : topiary

55. sequel : original

    A) frequent : turbulent

    B) subsequent : forever

    C) second : first

    D) serious : oblivious

Verbal Test #2 – Answers

1. D	20. A	39. A
2. B	21. C	40. B
3. A	22. B	41. D
4. C	23. A	42. C
5. A	24. A	43. C
6. C	25. D	44. D
7. B	26. C	45. A
8. D	27. B	46. C
9. B	28. B	47. A
10. C	29. B	48. B
11. A	30. A	49. A
12. D	31. D	50. D
13. D	32. B	51. C
14. B	33. C	52. B
15. A	34. A	53. D
16. B	35. B	54. A
17. C	36. C	55. C
18. D	37. C	
19. B	38. B	

Verbal Test #2 – Explanations

1. Answer: D
   Intimidate **is the same as** threaten.
   Diminish **is the same as** lessen.

2. Answer: B
   Poverty **is the opposite of** prosperity.
   Success **is the opposite of** failure.

3. Answer: A
   A blade **is a part of** a saw.
   A string **is a part of** a guitar.

4. Answer: C
   A cup and a mug **are types of** drinking vessels.
   A parallelogram and a hexagon **are types of** shapes.

5. Answer: A
   Independence **is the opposite of** dependence.
   Subjective **is the opposite of** objective.

6. Answer: C
   Contributor **is the same as** participant.
   Shopper **is the same as** consumer.

7. Answer: B
   A car **is a modern form of a** carriage.
   A computer **is a modern form of a** typewriter.

8. Answer: D
   A peak is **the opposite of** a base.
   Urban **is the opposite of** rural.

9. Answer: B
   Home **is the same as** dwelling.
   Perimeter **is the same as** border.

10. Answer: C

   Scissors **have the same motion and function as** shears.
   A knife **has the same motion and function** as a saw.

11. Answer: A

   Waxing **is the opposite of** waning.
   Dividing **is the opposite of** multiplying.

12. Answer: D

   Argument **is a lesser form of** feud
   Pout **is a lesser form of** tantrum.

13. Answer: D

   Income **is the same as** compensation.
   Bills **are the same as** expenses.

14. Answer: B

   Subtly **is the opposite of** blatantly.
   Insufficiently **is the opposite of** successfully.

15. Answer: A

   Papaya and watermelon **are both types of** fruit.
   Rainforest and swamp **are both types of** habitats.

16. Answer: B

   Balanced **is the opposite of** unequal.
   Typical **is the opposite of** eccentric.

17. Answer: C

   Accelerate **is the same as** expedite.
   Aspire **is the same as** strive.

18. Answer: D

   An archipelago **is made up of** islands.
   A constellation **is made up of** stars.

19. Answer: B

   A teaspoon **is used to measure** medicine (small amounts of liquid).
   A gallon **is used to measure** gasoline (large amounts of liquid).

20. Answer: A

Annihilate **is the same as** exterminate.

Disturb **is the same as** agitate.

21. Answer: C

The trumpet **is a type of** brass instrument

The clarinet **is a type of** woodwind instrument.

22. Answer: B

Spending **is the opposite of** saving.

Borrowing **is the opposite of** loaning.

23. Answer: A

Barrier **is the same as** blockade.

Boycott **is the same as** reject.

24. Answer: A

A hurricane **is the same** as a typhoon.

Arid **is the same as** dry.

25. Answer: D

Filthy **is the opposite of** sterile.

Disagree **is the opposite of** compromise.

26. Answer: C

Emblem **is the same as** symbol.

Conversation **is the same as** discourse.

27. Answer: B

Ceremoniously **is an example of an** adverb.

Timid **is an example of an** adjective.

28. Answer: B

A bird **builds a** nest.

A beaver **builds a** dam.

29. Answer: B

Agriculture **is the same as** farming.

Irrigation **is the same as** watering.

30. Answer: A

A pentagon **is a type of** polygon.

A scatter plot **is a type of** graph.

31. Answer: D

Import **is the opposite of** export.

Scarce **is the opposite of** plentiful.

32. Answer: B

A frog **is a type of** amphibian.

An owl **is a type of** bird.

33. Answer: C

Judicial and legislative **are both branches of** democratic government.

Army and navy **are both branches of** the U.S. military.

34. Answer: A

Lie **is the same as** fabricate.

Anger **is the same as** infuriate.

35. Answer: B

Enthrall **is the opposite of** bore.

Ponder **is the opposite of** forget.

36. Answer: C

Plumbing **transports** water.

Wiring **transports** electricity.

37. Answer: C

A paddle **moves a** kayak.

A sail **moves a** sailboat.

38. Answer: B

Condensation **is the opposite of** evaporation.

Comedy **is the opposite of** tragedy.

39. Answer: A

Nomadic **is the same as** migratory.

Barter **is the same as** trade.

40. Answer: B

Quadruple **means** four.

Quintuple **means** five.

41. Answer: D

Traditional **is the same as** classical.

Sponsor **is the same as** support.

42. Answer: C

Mono **is a prefix meaning** one.

Poly **is a prefix meaning** many.

43. Answer: C

A coach **has a similar role to** a teacher.

A baker **has a similar role to** a chef.

44. Answer: D

A monsoon **includes** rain.

A tornado **includes** wind.

45. Answer: A

A singer **entertains with** songs.

A comedian **entertains with** jokes.

46. Answer: C

Desert **is a type of** biomes.

Lettuce **is a type of** vegetable.

47. Answers: A

Connotation **is the same as** undertone.

Negligent **is the same as** inattentive.

48. Answers: B

Discern **is the opposite of** misinterpret.

Fruitful **is the opposite of** ineffective.

49. Answers: A

Conjecture **is the same as** assumption.

Probability **is the same as** likelihood.

50. Answers: D

A radius **is half of a** diameter.

A pint **is half of a** quart.

51. Answers: C

Spirit **is the same as** spunk.

Ajar **is the same as** unlatched.

52. Answers: B

Validate **is the opposite of** deny.

Astute **is the opposite of** foolish.

53. Answers: D

Rupture **is the same as** fissure.

Greedy **is the same as** avaricious.

54. Answers: A

Exclusion **is the opposite of** acceptance.

Lavish **is the opposite of** destitute.

55. Answers: C

The sequel **is after the** original.

The second **is after** first.

Quantitative Reasoning Test #2

55 Questions – 22 Minutes

1.

Column A	Column B
The number of faces on a sphere	The number of faces on a cube

A) Column A is greater.

B) Column B is greater.

C) Columns A and B are equal.

D) The relationship cannot be determined with the information given.

2.

Column A	Column B
The sum of the inside angles of an equilateral triangle	The largest angle in a right triangle

A) Column A is greater.

B) Column B is greater.

C) Columns A and B are equal.

D) The relationship cannot be determined with the information given.

3.

Column A	Column B
The sum of the first 3 prime numbers	The sum of the first 3 consecutive composite numbers beginning with 4

A) Column A is greater.

B) Column B is greater.

C) Columns A and B are equal.

D) The relationship cannot be determined with the information given.

4.

Column A	Column B
$18 - 3 - 3 - 3 - 3 - 3 - 3$	$18 \div 3$

A) Column A is greater.

B) Column B is greater.

C) Columns A and B are equal.

D) The relationship cannot be determined with the information given.

5.

Column A	Column B
$\dfrac{5}{6} \times \dfrac{2}{4}$	$\dfrac{5}{12}$

A) Column A is greater.

B) Column B is greater.

C) Columns A and B are equal.

D) The relationship cannot be determined with the information given.

6.

Column A	Column B
The number of degrees in a quadrilateral	The number of degrees in a triangle

A) Column A is greater.

B) Column B is greater.

C) Columns A and B are equal.

D) The relationship cannot be determined with the information given.

7.

Column A	Column B
$\frac{1}{7}$ of 56	$\frac{1}{8}$ of 24

A) Column A is greater.

B) Column B is greater.

C) Columns A and B are equal.

D) The relationship cannot be determined with the information given.

8. Data Set: 45, 46, 24, 32, 51

Column A	Column B
The median of the data set	The range of the data set

A) Column A is greater.

B) Column B is greater.

C) Columns A and B are equal.

D) The relationship cannot be determined with the information given.

9.

Column A	Column B
0^{12}	$(6 \times 0) \times (56 \div 7)$

A) Column A is greater.

B) Column B is greater.

C) Columns A and B are equal.

D) The relationship cannot be determined with the information given.

10.

Column A	Column B
$4 + \left(6 \times \frac{1}{10}\right)$	4.60

A) Column A is greater.

B) Column B is greater.

C) Columns A and B are equal.

D) The relationship cannot be determined with the information given.

11.

Column A	Column B
The next prime number after 32	The next odd number after 32

A) Column A is greater.

B) Column B is greater.

C) Columns A and B are equal.

D) The relationship cannot be determined with the information given.

12.

Column A	Column B
The mean of 6 test scores	The median of 6 test scores

A) Column A is greater.

B) Column B is greater.

C) Columns A and B are equal.

D) The relationship cannot be determined with the information given.

13.

Column A	Column B
8^2	4^4

A) Column A is greater.

B) Column B is greater.

C) Columns A and B are equal.

D) The relationship cannot be determined with the information given.

14.

Column A	Column B
The number of factors of 24	The number of factors of 13

A) Column A is greater.

B) Column B is greater.

C) Columns A and B are equal.

D) The relationship cannot be determined with the information given.

15.

Column A	Column B
25% of 32	50% of 64

A) Column A is greater.

B) Column B is greater.

C) Columns A and B are equal.

D) The relationship cannot be determined with the information given.

16. A package of three cupcakes costs $4.20. A package of two cookies costs $3.00.

Column A	Column B
Unit price of a cupcake	Unit price of a cookie

A) Column A is greater.

B) Column B is greater.

C) Columns A and B are equal.

D) The relationship cannot be determined with the information given.

17.

Column A	Column B
$200 + 7 + \left(8 \times \dfrac{1}{100}\right)$	207.08

A) Column A is greater.

B) Column B is greater.

C) Columns A and B are equal.

D) The relationship cannot be determined with the information given.

18.

Column A	Column B
$3 \times \dfrac{2}{3}$	$3 \div \dfrac{2}{3}$

A) Column A is greater.

B) Column B is greater.

C) Columns A and B are equal.

D) The relationship cannot be determined with the information given.

19.

Column A	Column B
13×19	24×11

A) Column A is greater.

B) Column B is greater.

C) Columns A and B are equal.

D) The relationship cannot be determined with the information given.

20.

Column A	Column B
$10^3 + 900 + 70 + 6$	$1000 + 9(100) + 7(10) + 6$

A) Column A is greater.

B) Column B is greater.

C) Columns A and B are equal.

D) The relationship cannot be determined with the information given.

21.

Column A	Column B
0.82	$\dfrac{82}{100}$

A) Column A is greater.

B) Column B is greater.

C) Columns A and B are equal.

D) The relationship cannot be determined with the information given.

22. Ray has 75 baseball and football cards in his collection. Sam has 100 baseball and football cards in his collection.

Column A	Column B
The number of football cards Ray has in his collection	The number of football cards Sam has in his collection

A) Column A is greater.

B) Column B is greater.

C) Columns A and B are equal.

D) The relationship cannot be determined with the information given.

23.

Column A	Column B
The sum of the angles in a trapezoid	The sum of the angles in a rhombus

A) Column A is greater.

B) Column B is greater.

C) Columns A and B are equal.

D) The relationship cannot be determined with the information given.

24.

Column A	Column B
The width of a rectangle with an area of 12 and a length of 6	The remainder of $46 \div 5$

A) Column A is greater.

B) Column B is greater.

C) Columns A and B are equal.

D) The relationship cannot be determined with the information given.

25.

Column A	Column B
The value of the underlined digit 325.4<u>9</u>	$9\left(\dfrac{1}{100}\right)$

A) Column A is greater.

B) Column B is greater.

C) Columns A and B are equal.

D) The relationship cannot be determined with the information given.

26.

Column A	Column B
$\sqrt{16}$	$4^2 \div 2$

A) Column A is greater.

B) Column B is greater.

C) Columns A and B are equal.

D) The relationship cannot be determined with the information given.

27.

Column A	Column B
The length of a side of an equilateral hexagon with a perimeter of 54 yards	The length of a triangle with a perimeter of 54 yards

A) Column A is greater.

B) Column B is greater.

C) Columns A and B are equal.

D) The relationship cannot be determined with the information given.

28.

Column A	Column B
Product of 52 and 4	The number of students in each group when 1000 of them are put into groups of 5

A) Column A is greater.

B) Column B is greater.

C) Columns A and B are equal.

D) The relationship cannot be determined with the information given.

29.

Column A	Column B
The value of b $29 \leq b$	The value of a $8 \times 2a$

A) Column A is greater.

B) Column B is greater.

C) Columns A and B are equal.

D) The relationship cannot be determined with the information given.

30.

Column A	Column B
$\frac{1}{6} \times 20$	$\frac{19}{3}$

A) Column A is greater.

B) Column B is greater.

C) Columns A and B are equal.

D) The relationship cannot be determined with the information given.

31.

Column A	Column B
Area of a right triangle with a height of 13 cm and a base of 4 cm	Perimeter of a square with 4.5 cm sides

A) Column A is greater.

B) Column B is greater.

C) Columns A and B are equal.

D) The relationship cannot be determined with the information given.

32. Tilly has 7 coins. Otto has 12 coins.

Column A	Column B
The value of Tilly's coins	The value of Otto's coins

A) Column A is greater.

B) Column B is greater.

C) Columns A and B are equal.

D) The relationship cannot be determined with the information given.

33.

Column A	Column B
The total length of 4 pieces of rope with each rope being 4.25 inches long	$1 \frac{1}{2}$ feet

A) Column A is greater.

B) Column B is greater.

C) Columns A and B are equal.

D) The relationship cannot be determined with the information given.

34.

Column A	Column B
The value of 7 quarters, 3 dimes, 20 nickels, 3 pennies	The value of 10 quarters, 2 dimes, 40 nickels, 3 pennies

A) Column A is greater.

B) Column B is greater.

C) Columns A and B are equal.

D) The relationship cannot be determined with the information given.

35. There is a spinner with equal parts, numbers from 1-6.

Column A	Column B
The probability of spinning an odd number.	The probability of spinning an even number.

A) Column A is greater.

B) Column B is greater.

C) Columns A and B are equal.

D) The relationship cannot be determined with the information given.

36.

Column A	Column B
The value of a $-7 \times 8 = a$	The value of b $-7 \times -8 = b$

A) Column A is greater.

B) Column B is greater.

C) Columns A and B are equal.

D) The relationship cannot be determined with the information given.

37.

Column A	Column B
The sum of factors of 24	The sum of factors of 27

A) Column A is greater.

B) Column B is greater.

C) Columns A and B are equal.

D) The relationship cannot be determined with the information given.

38.

Column A	Column B
$8\frac{3}{5}$	$\frac{13}{2} \div \frac{1}{2}$

A) Column A is greater.

B) Column B is greater.

C) Columns A and B are equal.

D) The relationship cannot be determined with the information given.

39.

Column A	Column B
30 miles.	30 kilometers.

A) Column A is greater.

B) Column B is greater.

C) Columns A and B are equal.

D) The relationship cannot be determined with the information given.

40.

Column A	Column B
$\sqrt{144} + \sqrt{64}$	4×5

A) Column A is greater.

B) Column B is greater.

C) Columns A and B are equal.

D) The relationship cannot be determined with the information given.

41.

Column A   **Column B**

The value of x

1	2	3	4
1.5	3	4.5	x

The value of y

3	4	5	6
y	8	10	12

A) Column A is greater.

B) Column B is greater.

C) Columns A and B are equal.

D) The relationship cannot be determined with the information given.

42.

Column A	Column B
The value of x $6x - 30 = 6$	The value of x $8x - 14 = 18$

A) Column A is greater.

B) Column B is greater.

C) Columns A and B are equal.

D) The relationship cannot be determined with the information given.

43.

Column A	Column B
$\frac{1}{3}$ of 24	$\frac{1}{8}$ of 64

A) Column A is greater.

B) Column B is greater.

C) Columns A and B are equal.

D) The relationship cannot be determined with the information given.

44.

Column A	Column B
The denominator when $\frac{3}{45}$ is reduced to its lowest terms	The denominator when $\frac{12}{48}$ is reduced to its lowest terms

A) Column A is greater.

B) Column B is greater.

C) Columns A and B are equal.

D) The relationship cannot be determined with the information given.

45.

Column A				Column B			
The value of x				The value of y			
3	6	9	15	6	12	24	48
15	x	45	75	y	48	96	592

A) Column A is greater.

B) Column B is greater.

C) Columns A and B are equal.

D) The relationship cannot be determined with the information given.

46.

Column A	Column B
The number of outfit combinations that can be created with 4 shirts and 3 pairs of pants	The number of outfit combinations that can be created with 5 shirts and 2 pairs of pants

A) Column A is greater.

B) Column B is greater.

C) Columns A and B are equal.

D) The relationship cannot be determined with the information given.

47.

Column A	Column B
$12 + 1^{32}$	$(5 \times 3) - 2$

A) Column A is greater.

B) Column B is greater.

C) Columns A and B are equal.

D) The relationship cannot be determined with the information given.

48.

There are a total of 100 cupcakes at the wedding. 50 are red velvet, 20 are salted caramel, and 30 are vanilla.

Column A	Column B
The ratio of red velvet cupcakes to salted caramel cupcakes	The ratio of red velvet cupcakes to vanilla cupcakes

A) Column A is greater.

B) Column B is greater.

C) Columns A and B are equal.

D) The relationship cannot be determined with the information given.

49.

Column A	Column B
10% of 180	2% of 800

A) Column A is greater.

B) Column B is greater.

C) Columns A and B are equal.

D) The relationship cannot be determined with the information given.

50. Store A and Store B both sell hoodies for $36.00.

Column A	Column B
The average cost of per hoodie at Store A with a buy one get one free promotion	The cost of a hoodie at Store B with a 25% off promotion

A) Column A is greater.

B) Column B is greater.

C) Columns A and B are equal.

D) The relationship cannot be determined with the information given.

51.

Column A	Column B
$\frac{24}{2} + \frac{18}{3}$	$\frac{(6 \times 6)}{2}$

A) Column A is greater.

B) Column B is greater.

C) Columns A and B are equal.

D) The relationship cannot be determined with the information given.

52.

Column A	Column B
2 hours 15 minutes	124 minutes

A) Column A is greater.

B) Column B is greater.

C) Columns A and B are equal.

D) The relationship cannot be determined with the information given.

53.

Column A	Column B
$325 \div 8$	$542 \div 9$

A) Column A is greater.

B) Column B is greater.

C) Columns A and B are equal.

D) The relationship cannot be determined with the information given.

54.

Column A	Column B
The value of 12 dimes and one nickel	The value of five quarters

A) Column A is greater.

B) Column B is greater.

C) Columns A and B are equal.

D) The relationship cannot be determined with the information given.

55.

Column A	Column B
The ratio of vowels in the word watermelon to all the letters in the word watermelon	The ratio of consonants in the word watermelon to all the letters in the word watermelon

A) Column A is greater.

B) Column B is greater.

C) Columns A and B are. equal.

D) The relationship cannot be determined with the information given.

Quantitative Test #2 – Answers

1. B	20. C	39. A
2. A	21. C	40. C
3. B	22. D	41. C
4. B	23. C	42. A
5. C	24. A	43. C
6. A	25. C	44. A
7. A	26. B	45. A
8. A	27. B	46. A
9. C	28. A	47. C
10. C	29. D	48. A
11. A	30. B	49. A
12. D	31. A	50. B
13. B`	32. D	51. C
14. A	33. B	52. A
15. B	34. B	53. B
16. B	35. C	54. C
17. C	36. B	55. B
18. B	37. A	
19. B	38. B	

Quantitative Test #2 - Explanations

1. **B**

Column A	Column B
The number of faces on a sphere	The number of faces on a cube
1	6

2. **A**

Column A	Column B
The sum of the inside angles of an equilateral triangle	The largest angle in a right triangle
An equilateral triangle has three equal angles. Each is 60 degrees because 60+60+60 = 180	90 degrees

3. **B**

Column A	Column B
The sum of the first 3 prime numbers	The sum of the first 3 consecutive numbers beginning with 4
2 + 3 + 5	4 + 5 + 6

4. **B**

Column A	Column B
$18 - 3 - 3 - 3 - 3 - 3 - 3$	$18 \div 3$
$18 - (3 \ six \ times)$	6
$18 - 18$	
0	

5. **C**

Column A	Column B
$\dfrac{5}{6} \times \dfrac{2}{4}$	$\dfrac{5}{12}$
$\dfrac{5}{6} \times \dfrac{2}{4} = \dfrac{10}{24} \rightarrow \dfrac{5}{12}$	

6. **A**

Column A	Column B
The number of degrees in a quadrilateral	The number of degrees in a triangle
360	180

7. **A**

Column A	Column B
$\dfrac{1}{7}$ of 56	$\dfrac{1}{8}$ of 24
$\dfrac{56}{7} = 8$	$\dfrac{24}{8} = 3$

8. **A**

   Data Set: 45, 46, 24, 32, 51

Column A	Column B
The median of the data set	The range of the data set
24, 32, 45, 46, 51	$51 - 24 = 27$
~~24, 32,~~ 45, ~~46, 51~~	
45	

9. **C**

Column A	Column B
0^{12}	$(6 \times 0) \times (56 \div 7)$
0	Anything $\times$ 0 is 0

10. **C**

Column A	Column B
$4 + \left(6 \times \frac{1}{10} \right)$	4.60
$4\frac{6}{10} \to 4.6$	

11. **A**

Column A	Column B
The next prime number after 32	The next odd number after 32
37	33

12. **D**

Column A	Column B
The mean of 6 test scores	The median of 6 test scores
There is no information on the scores, so the answer cannot be determined.	

13. **B**

Column A	Column B
8^2	4^4
8×8	$4 \times 4 \times 4 \times 4$
64	256

14. **A**

Column A	Column B
The number of factors of 24	The number of factors of 13
24 has many factors and is not prime. 24 has more factors than 13 has.	13 is a prime number. The only factors are 1 and 13.

15. **B**

Column A	Column B
25% of 32	50% of 64
Less than 32	32

16. **B**
A package of three cupcakes costs $4.20. A package of two cookies costs $3.00.

Column A	Column B
Unit price of a cupcake	Unit price of a cookie
$4.20 \div 3$	$3.00 \div 2$
$42 \div 3 = 14$	1.50
1.40	

17. **C**

Column A	Column B
$200 + 7 + \left(8 \times \dfrac{1}{100}\right)$	207.08
$207\dfrac{8}{100} \rightarrow 207.08$	

18. **B**

Column A	Column B
$3 \times \dfrac{2}{3}$	$3 \div \dfrac{2}{3}$
$\dfrac{3}{1} \times \dfrac{2}{3} = \dfrac{6}{3} = 2$	$\dfrac{3}{1} \times \dfrac{3}{2} = \dfrac{9}{2} = 4\dfrac{1}{2}$

19. **B**

Column A	Column B
13×19	24×11
$13 \times 20 = 260$	$24 \times 10 = 240$
$13 \times 19 = 260 - 13$	$24 \times 11 = 240 + 24$
247	264

20. **C**

Column A	Column B
$10^3 + 900 + 70 + 6$	$1000 + 9(100) + 7(10) + 6$
$1000 + 900 + 70 + 6$	$1000 + 900 + 70 + 6$

21. **C**

Column A	Column B
0.82	$\dfrac{82}{100}$
$\dfrac{82}{100}$	

22. **D**

Ray has 75 baseball and football cards in his collection. One third of his collection is baseball cards. Sam has 100 baseball and football cards in his collection.

Column A	Column B
The number of football cards Ray has in his collection	The number of football cards Sam has in his collection
25	No information given

23. **C**

Column A	Column B
The sum of the angles in a trapezoid	The sum of the angles in a rhombus
4-sided figure = 360 degrees	4 -sided figure = 360 degrees

24. A

Column A	Column B
The width of a rectangle with an area of 12 and a length of 6 Area = length × width 12= 6 × 2 2	The remainder of 46 ÷ 5 5 × 9 = 45 1 remaining

25. C

Column A	Column B
The value of the underlined digit 325.4<u>9</u> 0.09	$9\left(\dfrac{1}{100}\right)$ $\dfrac{9}{100} \rightarrow 0.09$

26. B

Column A	Column B
$\sqrt{16}$ 4	$4^2 \div 2$ 16 ÷ 2 8

27. B

Column A	Column B
The length of a side of an equilateral hexagon with a perimeter of 54 yards Divide 54 by 6 sides	The length of a triangle with a perimeter of 54 yards Divide 54 by 3 sides Sides are larger because the 54 is being divided into fewer parts

28. A

Column A	Column B
Product of 52 and 4	The number of students in each group when 1000 of them are put into groups of 5
52×4	$1000 \div 5$
$50 \times 4 = 200$	200
$2 \times 4 = 8$	
208	

29. D

Column A	Column B
The value of b	The value of a
$29 \leq b$	$8 \times 2a$
Greater than 29	Unknown

30. B

Column A	Column B
$\dfrac{1}{6} \times 20$	$\dfrac{19}{3}$
$\dfrac{20}{6} = 3\dfrac{2}{6}$ or $3\dfrac{1}{3}$	$\dfrac{19}{3} = 6\dfrac{1}{3}$

31. A

Column A	Column B
Area of a right triangle with a height of 13 cm and a base of 4 cm	Perimeter of a square with 4.5 cm sides
$Area = \dfrac{1}{2}\ base \times height$	$Perimeter = 4.5 \times 4$
	$4.5 \times 2 = 9$
$Area = \dfrac{1}{2}(4) \times 13$	$9 \times 2 = 18$
26	

32. **D**

Tilly has 7 coins. Otto has 12 coins.

Column A	Column B
The value of Tilly's coins Unknown *Coins could be all pennies or all quarters. Even though Tilly has more coins, the value could be less than Otto's value.*	The value of Otto's coins Unknown

33. **B**

Column A	Column B
The total length of 4 pieces of rope with each rope being 4.25 inches long $$4 \times 4.25 = 17 \; inches$$	$1 \frac{1}{2}$ feet $$1 \; foot = 12 \; inches$$ $$\frac{1}{2} foot = 6 \; inches$$ $$1 \frac{1}{2} \; feet = 18 \; inches$$

34. **B**

Column A	Column B
The value of 7 quarters, 3 dimes, 20 nickels, 3 pennies 1 more dime = +10 cents	The value of 10 quarters, 2 dimes, 40 nickels, 3 pennies 3 more quarters = +75 cents 20 more nickels = + 100 cents

Do not count up the total value! Just compare!

35. **C**

There is a spinner with equal parts, numbers from 1-6.

Column A	Column B
The probability of spinning an odd number	The probability of spinning an even number
1, 3, or 5	2, 4, or 6
$\dfrac{3}{6}$	$\dfrac{3}{6}$

36. **B**

Column A	Column B
The value of a	The value of b
$-7 \times 8 = a$	$-7 \times -8 = b$
-56	56
	In multiplication, two negatives cancel each other out (a negative × a negative is a positive)

37. **A**

Column A	Column B
The sum of factors of 24	The sum of factors of 27
Factors: 1, 24, 3, 8, 4, 6, 2, 12	Factors: 1, 27, 3, 9
No need to add them. There are many more factors so the sum will be greater.	

38. **B**

Column A	Column B
$8\frac{3}{5}$	$\dfrac{13}{2} \div \dfrac{1}{2}$
	$\dfrac{13}{2} \times \dfrac{2}{1} = \dfrac{26}{2} = 13$

39. **A**

Column A	Column B
Car A drives 30 miles.	Car B drives 30 kilometers.
	Kilometers are shorter than miles. (A 5k race is about 3 miles).

40. **C**

Column A	Column B
$\sqrt{144} + \sqrt{64}$	4×5
12 + 8	20
20	

41. **C**

Column A	Column B
The value of x	The value of y

1	2	3	4
1.5	3	4.5	x

3	4	5	6
y	8	10	12

Pattern: Add 1.5

$4.5 + 1.5 = 6$

Pattern: Add 2

$8 - 2 = 6$

42. **A**

Column A	Column B
The value of x	The value of x
$6x - 30 = 6$	$8x - 14 = 18$
$6x = 36$	$8x = 32$
$x = 6$	$x = 4$

43. **C**

Column A	Column B
$\frac{1}{3}$ of 24	$\frac{1}{8}$ of 64
$\frac{1}{3} \times 24 = \frac{24}{3}$	$\frac{1}{8} \times 64 = \frac{64}{8}$
$\frac{24}{3} = 8$	$\frac{64}{8} = 8$

Remember: In math, of means multiply!

44. **A**

Column A	Column B
The denominator when $\frac{3}{45}$ is reduced to its lowest terms	The denominator when $\frac{12}{48}$ is reduced to its lowest terms
$\frac{3}{45} \rightarrow \frac{3 \div 3}{45 \div 3} \rightarrow \frac{1}{15}$	$\frac{12}{48} \rightarrow \frac{12 \div 12}{48 \div 12} \rightarrow \frac{1}{4}$
15	4

45. **A**

Column A	Column B
The value of x	The value of y

3	6	9	15
15	x	45	75

6	12	24	48
y	48	96	592

Column A

Pattern:
+ 15 OR top value times 5

$6 \times 5 = 30$
30

Column B

Pattern:
Double the previous value OR
top value times 4

$6 \times 4 = 24$
24

46. **A**

Column A	Column B
The number of outfit combinations that can be created with 4 shirts and 3 pairs of pants	The number of outfit combinations that can be created with 5 shirts and 2 pairs of pants
4×3	5×2
12	10

47. **C**

Column A	Column B
$12 + 1^{32}$	$(5 \times 3) - 2$
$12 + 1$	$15 - 2$
13	13

48. **A**

There are a total of 100 cupcakes at the wedding. 50 are red velvet, 20 are salted caramel, and 30 are vanilla.

Column A	Column B
The ratio of red velvet cupcakes to salted caramel cupcakes	The ratio of red velvet cupcakes to vanilla cupcakes
$50:20$	$50:30$
$\dfrac{50}{20} \rightarrow \dfrac{5}{2}$	$\dfrac{50}{30} \rightarrow \dfrac{5}{3}$
More red velvet per salted caramel than per vanilla	

49. **A**

Column A	Column B
10% of 180	2% of 800
To get 10%, divide by 10 18	10% = 80 1% = 8 2% = 16

50. **B**

Store A and Store B both sell hoodies for $36.00.

Column A	Column B
The average cost of per hoodie at Store A with a buy one get one free promotion	The cost of a hoodie at Store B with a 25% off promotion
36 for 2 hoodies 18 each Half off the original price	Only a quarter off the original price

51. **C**

Column A	Column B
$\dfrac{24}{2} + \dfrac{18}{3}$	$\dfrac{(6 \times 6)}{2}$
$12 + 6 = 18$	$\dfrac{36}{2} = 18$

52. **A**

Column A	Column B
2 hours 15 minutes	124 minutes
1 hour = 60 minutes 2 hours = 120 minutes	
120 +15 = 135 minutes	

53. **B**

Column A	Column B
$325 \div 8$	$542 \div 9$
Estimate: $320 \div 8 = 40$	Estimate: $540 \div 9 = 60$

54. **C**

Column A	Column B
The value of 12 dimes and one nickel	The value of five quarters
$12 \times 10 + 5$ $120 + 5$ 125	25×5 125

55. **B**

Column A	Column B
The ratio of vowels in the word watermelon to all the letters in the word watermelon	The ratio of consonants in the word watermelon to all the letters in the word watermelon
4 vowels : 10 letters	6 consonants : 10 letters

Practice Test #3

Verbal Test #3

55 Questions – 22 Minutes

1. mundane : fun

   A) quick : speedy

   B) regardless : despite

   C) substantial : insignificant

   D) sojourning : traveling

2. insinuate : allude

   A) fret : fritter

   B) investigate : populate

   C) opinionated : infiltrate

   D) inundate : flood

3. terrified : afraid

   A) turbulent : trembling

   B) quite : quiet

   C) frequent : fraudulent

   D) garage : garbage

4. kilometer : meter

   A) inchworm : centimeter

   B) millimeter : hand

   C) yard : foot

   D) kiloliter : liter

5. option : obligation

   A) freedom : choices

   B) blade : sword

   C) pain : pleasure

   D) trim : grout

6. surgeon : doctor

    A) actor : entertainer

    B) server : dentist

    C) teacher : scientist

    D) troublemaker : trainer

7. gripping : pliers

    A) spear : anvil

    B) bolt : wrench

    C) frame : caliper

    D) cutting : clippers

8. notorious : infamous

    A) notable : unimportant

    B) implore : plead

    C) whimsical : fiddle

    D) stagnant : sodden

9. sheltered : exposed

    A) trip : stinging

    B) love : hate

    C) fanciful : fainting

    D) trough : rough

10. kid : goat

    A) foal : gosling

    B) plant : parade

    C) kit : fox

    D) mare : lair

11. modify : adjust

   A) shirk : avoid

   B) patient : impulsive

   C) thoughtful : transpose

   D) violent : shameful

12. astronaut : explores

   A) biologist : sleeps

   B) butcher : climbs

   C) translator : constructs

   D) architect : designs

13. bliss : pleasure

   A) trafficking : whittling

   B) climax : height

   C) jokester : monitor

   D) brokenness : tropical

14. slide : trombone

   A) reed : clarinet

   B) horn : deafening

   C) timpani : silent

   D) mouthpiece : marimba

15. random : arbitrary

   A) divergent : divulging

   B) insurgent : innovator

   C) simultaneously : concurrently

   D) crustation : damaging

16. free : limited

    A) jacket : coat

    B) frivolous : thoughtful

    C) glove : hand

    D) boots : shoes

17. blender : mixer

    A) spatula : fork

    B) spreader : tongs

    C) springform : cooker

    D) spoon : ladle

18. mellow : calm

    A) intensify : aggravate

    B) lineate : fellow

    C) mystify: transform

    D) magnify : glass

19. debt : surplus

    A) pale : pallor

    B) distributing : collecting

    C) potentate : palisade

    D) chastise : fledgling

20. moon : phases

    A) gibbous : autumn

    B) seasonal : eclipse

    C) time : years

    D) miniscule : century

21. spine : book

   A) prong : fork

   B) rhapsody : ransom

   C) quilted : quaint

   D) shimmery : silken

22. revenge : forgiveness

   A) apron : toboggan

   B) litigation : litany

   C) jargon : colloquial

   D) belittle : encourage

23. crush : trample

   A) might : conflagrate

   B) mull : contemplate

   C) catatonic : mansions

   D) espionage : majestic

24. actors : troupe

   A) communicate : hiccup

   B) hostage : consider

   C) hamper : hinder

   D) instrumentalists : band

25. grate : great

   A) familiarize : frontal

   B) notion : idealize

   C) daze : days

   D) palpitation : mitigate

26. despondent : disheartened

    A) trial : recognize

    B) devour : absorb

    C) vaporize : witty

    D) harness : think

27. nimble : awkward

    A) frightened : transmigration

    B) lullaby : trailer

    C) harrowing : harvesting

    D) slacker : overachiever

28. transport : move

    A) span : breadth

    B) retie : unload

    C) underwhelm : immature

    D) subpar : inaccurate

29. null : void

    A) feet : hurt

    B) collateral : irreverent

    C) template : pattern

    D) leg : knee

30. river : lake

    A) botanist : animals

    B) wicker : friendliness

    C) divan : curls

    D) roots : tree

31. attributes : characteristics

   A) alternate : gargantuan

   B) docile : tame

   C) honorable : lever

   D) laughable : laudable

32. complementary : unrelated

   A) reciprocal : purification

   B) rationing : coordinated

   C) polyhedron : protractor

   D) wary : careless

33. accommodation : asphyxiation

   A) fossilize : sterilize

   B) prism : dependent

   C) hypotenuse : rebate

   D) scaffolding : scalene

34. wince : cringe

   A) pyramid : infuriate

   B) composite : cylindrical

   C) implore : beg

   D) analyze : welcome

35. Isosceles : equilateral

   A) relativity : radical

   B) rhombus : trapezoid

   C) transitory : appositive

   D) divisible : duplicate

36. yearn : ache

    A) foul : rat

    B) tendency : mode

    C) revolutionary : imitator

    D) wrath : fury

37. counsel : advise

    A) coordinates : operations

    B) believe : trust

    C) position : metallic

    D) location : grunge

38. symmetrical : disproportionate

    A) transmutation : salutation

    B) tessellation : edification

    C) complex : simple

    D) absolve : petition

39. lawyer : law

    A) botanist : plants

    B) pecan : troll

    C) escapade : saga

    D) fostering : lacquer

40. detach : disassemble

    A) odyssey : book

    B) murky : muddy

    C) gnome : stilt

    D) functioning : refuting

41. magnitude : degree

    A) exponential : slow

    B) mean : average

    C) proportional : shape

    D) slipshod : superior

42. guitarist : pianist

    A) guide : wilderness

    B) artist : painter

    C) biologist : chemist

    D) teacher : student

43. correspond : deviate

    A) magma : lava

    B) casserole : pasta

    C) liquidate : stupefy

    D) interior : peripheral

44. repairman : appliances

    A) stylist : hair

    B) symbiotic : alien

    C) nail : hammer

    D) attendant : pilot

45. doe : buck

    A) vixen : cock

    B) saber : tooth

    C) hen : rooster

    D) puppy : dog

46. eighties : nineties

   A) cinnamon : spice

   B) hazel : color

   C) transformable : unstoppable

   D) February : March

47. heroic : savior

   A) sleuth : dreamily

   B) rhapsody : secretive

   C) deviant : criminal

   D) sweltering : simmering

48. reflection : contemplation

   A) saunter : shriek

   B) shrew : platypus

   C) soliloquy : almond

   D) apex : top

49. merchandise : warehouse

   A) filibuster : theatrical

   B) slather : restraint

   C) milk : refrigerator

   D) stringent : voluptuous

50. equitable : disproportionate

   A) idea : intangible

   B) soaked : dry

   C) canon : compilation

   D) topographic : unabridged

51. pharmacist : medicines

    A) shaman : trumpeter

    B) hitherto : strategy

    C) bibliographical : saturated

    D) photographer : cameras

52. melancholy : cheerful

    A) phlegmatic : profound

    B) drizzle : pour

    C) objective : optimistic

    D) epilogue : conclusion

53. anthology : compilation

    A) trilogy : acknowledgements

    B) pineapple : orange

    C) ruin : decimate

    D) anatomy : body

54. huntress : weapon

    A) gold : stenographer

    B) mocking : telegraph

    C) bad : cynical

    D) diver : water

55. snob : haughty

    A) appease : calm

    B) stampeded : protruded

    C) steel : steal

    D) brat : disrespectful

Verbal Test #3 – Answers

1. C	20. C	39. A
2. D	21. A	40. B
3. A	22. D	41. B
4. D	23. B	42. C
5. C	24. D	43. D
6. A	25. C	44. A
7. D	26. B	45. C
8. B	27. D	46. D
9. B	28. A	47. C
10. C	29. C	48. D
11. A	30. D	49. C
12. D	31. B	50. B
13. B	32. D	51. D
14. A	33. A	52. B
15. C	34. C	53. C
16. B	35. B	54. D
17. D	36. D	55. D
18. A	37. B	
19. B	38. C	

Verbal Test #3 – Explanations

1. Answer: C
   Mundane **is the opposite of** fun.
   Substantial **is the opposite of** insignificant.

2. Answer: D
   Insinuate **is the same as** allude.
   Inundate **is the same as** flood.

3. Answer: A
   Terrified **is a higher degree of** afraid.
   Turbulent **is a higher degree of** trembling.

4. Answer: D
   A kilometer **is 1000** meters.
   A kiloliter **is 1000** liters.

5. Answer: C
   Option **is the opposite of** obligation.
   Pain **is the opposite of** pleasure.

6. Answer: A
   A surgeon **is a type of** doctor.
   An actor **is a type of** entertainer.

7. Answer: D
   Gripping **is the function of** pliers.
   Cutting **is the function of** clippers.

8. Answer: B
   Notorious **is the same as** infamous.
   Implore **is the same as** plead.

9. Answer: B
   Sheltered **is the opposite of** exposed.
   Love **is the opposite of** hate.

10. Answer: C
    A kid **is a baby** goat.
    A kit **is a baby** fox.

11. Answer: A
    Modify **is the same as** adjust.
    Shirk **is the same as** avoid.

12. Answer: D
    An astronaut **is a person who** explores.
    An architect **is a person who** designs.

13. Answer: B
    Bliss **is a higher form of** pleasure.
    Climax **is a higher form of** height.

14. Answer: A
    The slide **is a part of** a trombone.
    The reed **is a part of** a clarinet.

15. Answer: C
    Random **is the same as** arbitrary.
    Simultaneously **is the same as** concurrently.

16. Answer: B
    Free **is the opposite of** limited.
    Frivolous **is the opposite of** thoughtful.

17. Answer: D
    A blender **has a similar function to** a mixer.
    A spoon **has a similar function to** a ladle.

18. Answer: A
    Mellow **is the same as** calm.
    Intensify **is the same as** aggravate.

19. Answer: B
    Debt **is the opposite of** surplus.
    Distributing **is the opposite of** collecting.

20. Answer: C
    The moon **is measured in** phases.
    Time **is measured in** years.

21. Answer: A

    A spine **is a part of** a book.

    A prong **is a part of** a fork.

22. Answer: D

    Revenge **is the opposite of** forgiveness.

    Belittle **is the opposite of** encourage.

23. Answer: B

    Crush **is the same as** trample.

    Mull **is the same as** contemplate.

24. Answer: D

    Actors **are members of** a troupe.

    Instrumentalists **are members of** a band.

25. Answer: C

    Red and read **are homophones**.

    Daze and days **are homophones**.

26. Answer: B

    Despondent **is the same as** disheartened.

    Devour **is the same as** absorb.

27. Answer: D

    Nimble **is the opposite of** awkward.

    Slacker **is the opposite of** overachiever.

28. Answer: A

    Transport **is the same as** move.

    Span **is the same as** breadth.

29. Answer: C

    Null **is the same as** void.

    Template **is the same as** pattern.

30. Answer: D

    A river **feeds into a** lake.

    Roots **feed into a** tree.

31. Answer: B

    Attributes **are the same as** characteristics.

    Docile **is the same as** tame.

32. Answer: D

Complementary **is the opposite of** unrelated.
Wary **is the opposite of** careless.

33. Answer: A

Accommodation **has the same suffix as** asphyxiation.
Fossilize **has the same suffix as** sterilize.

34. Answer: C

Wince **is the same as** cringe.
Implore **is the same as** beg.

35. Answer: B

Isosceles and equilateral **are types of** triangles.
Rhombus and trapezoid **are types of** quadrilaterals.

36. Answer: D

Yearn **is the same as** ache.
Wrath **is the same as** fury.

37. Answer: B

Notify **is the same as** advise.
Believe **is the same as** trust.

38. Answer: C

Symmetrical **is the opposite of** disproportionate.
Complex **is the opposite of** simple.

39. Answer: A

A lawyer **studies** law.
A botanist **studies** plants.

40. Answer: B

Detach **is the same as** disassemble.
Murky **is the same as** muddy.

41. Answer: B

Magnitude **is the same as** degree.
Mean **is the same as** average.

42. Answer: C

A guitarist and pianist **are both types of** instrumentalists.

A biologist and chemist **are both types of** scientists.

43. Answer: D

Correspond **is the opposite of** deviate.

Interior **is the opposite of** peripheral.

44. Answer: A

A repairman **works on** appliances.

A hairdresser **works on** hair.

45. Answer: C

Doe and buck **are the female and male names of** deer.

Hen and rooster **are the female and male names of** chicken.

46. Answer: D

Eighties **come before** nineties.

February **comes before** March.

47. Answer: C

Heroic **describes** a savior.

Deviant **describes** criminal.

48. Answers: D

Reflection **is the same as** contemplation.

Apex **is the same as** top.

49. Answers: C

Merchandise **is kept in** the warehouse.

Milk **is kept in** a refrigerator.

50. Answers: B

Equitable **is the opposite of** disproportionate.

Soaked **is the opposite of** dry.

51. Answers: D

A pharmacist **manages** medicines.

A photographer **manages** cameras.

52. Answers: B

Melancholy **is the opposite of** cheerful.

Drizzle **is the opposite of** pour.

53. Answers: C

   Anthology **is the same as** compilation.
   Ruin **is the same as** decimate.

54. Answers: D

   A huntress **needs** a weapon.
   A diver **needs** water.

55. Answers: D

   A snob **is described as** haughty.
   A brat **is described as** disrespectful.

Quantitative Reasoning Test #3

55 Questions – 22 Minutes

1.

Column A	Column B
The perimeter of a regular hexagon with sides that are 8 inches long	The perimeter of a pentagon with sides that are 8 inches long

A) Column A is greater.

B) Column B is greater.

C) Columns A and B are equal.

D) The relationship cannot be determined with the information given.

2.

Column A	Column B
One interior angle of an equilateral triangle	One interior angle of a rectangle

A) Column A is greater.

B) Column B is greater.

C) Columns A and B are equal.

D) The relationship cannot be determined with the information given.

3.

Column A	Column B
5^2	$\sqrt{25}$

A) Column A is greater.

B) Column B is greater.

C) Columns A and B are equal.

D) The relationship cannot be determined with the information given.

4.

Column A	Column B
$8 + 8 + 8 + 8$	$4^2 \times 2$

A) Column A is greater.

B) Column B is greater.

C) Columns A and B are equal.

D) The relationship cannot be determined with the information given.

5.

Column A	Column B
$\dfrac{3}{4} \times \dfrac{4}{3}$	$\dfrac{4}{16} \times \dfrac{2}{3}$

A) Column A is greater.

B) Column B is greater.

C) Columns A and B are equal.

D) The relationship cannot be determined with the information given.

6.

Column A	Column B
An acute angle	A right angle

A) Column A is greater.

B) Column B is greater.

C) Columns A and B are equal.

D) The relationship cannot be determined with the information given.

7.

Column A	Column B
$\frac{1}{5}$ of 20	$\frac{1}{9}$ of 36

A) Column A is greater.

B) Column B is greater.

C) Columns A and B are equal.

D) The relationship cannot be determined with the information given.

8.

Column A	Column B
The number of factors of 21	The number of factors of 23

A) Column A is greater.

B) Column B is greater.

C) Columns A and B are equal.

D) The relationship cannot be determined with the information given.

9.

Column A	Column B
The value of a $2a = 14$	The value of a $6 + a = 16$

A) Column A is greater.

B) Column B is greater.

C) Columns A and B are equal.

D) The relationship cannot be determined with the information given.

10.

There are 3 boys and 5 girls in group A. There are 2 boys and 11 girls in group B.

Column A	Column B
The ratio of boys to girls in group A	The ratio of boys to girls in group B

A) Column A is greater.

B) Column B is greater.

C) Columns A and B are equal.

D) The relationship cannot be determined with the information given.

11.

Column A	Column B
The smallest factor of 45	The smallest factor of 5

A) Column A is greater.

B) Column B is greater.

C) Columns A and B are equal.

D) The relationship cannot be determined with the information given.

12.

Column A	Column B
The range of 8 different numbers	The mode of 8 different numbers

A) Column A is greater.

B) Column B is greater.

C) Columns A and B are equal.

D) The relationship cannot be determined with the information given.

13.

Column A	Column B
The value of x	The value of x
$9x = 72$	$\frac{72}{x} = 9$

A) Column A is greater.

B) Column B is greater.

C) Columns A and B are equal.

D) The relationship cannot be determined with the information given.

14.

Column A	Column B
$4^2 + 4^2$	4^4

A) Column A is greater.

B) Column B is greater.

C) Columns A and B are equal.

D) The relationship cannot be determined with the information given.

15. Jane has two 16-inch pizzas. One pizza was 8 equal slices. One pizza has 12 equal slices.

Column A	Column B
The pizza with 8 slices	The pizza with 12 slices

A) Column A is greater.

B) Column B is greater.

C) Columns A and B are equal.

D) The relationship cannot be determined with the information given.

16.

Column A	Column B
The mode of: 8, 8, 6, 4, 2, 3, 5	The range of: 8, 8, 6, 4, 2, 3, 5

A) Column A is greater.

B) Column B is greater.

C) Columns A and B are equal.

D) The relationship cannot be determined with the information given.

17. A packet of four pencils costs $0.80. Individual pencils cost a quarter.

Column A	Column B
Price of a pencil in the pack	Price of a single pencil

A) Column A is greater.

B) Column B is greater.

C) Columns A and B are equal.

D) The relationship cannot be determined with the information given.

18.

Column A	Column B
$30 + 6 + \left(4 \times \dfrac{1}{10}\right)$	Three tens, 6 ones, 4 tenths

A) Column A is greater.

B) Column B is greater.

C) Columns A and B are equal.

D) The relationship cannot be determined with the information given.

19.

Column A	Column B
$\dfrac{5}{12} \times \dfrac{2}{3}$	$\dfrac{5}{12} \div \dfrac{2}{3}$

A) Column A is greater.

B) Column B is greater.

C) Columns A and B are equal.

D) The relationship cannot be determined with the information given.

20.

Column A	Column B
$3^2 + 1^{15}$	$3^2 + 1^9$

A) Column A is greater.

B) Column B is greater.

C) Columns A and B are equal.

D) The relationship cannot be determined with the information given.

21.

Column A	Column B
$10^4 \div 50$	$10^2 \times 200$

A) Column A is greater.

B) Column B is greater.

C) Columns A and B are equal.

D) The relationship cannot be determined with the information given.

22.

Column A	Column B
0.42	0.420

A) Column A is greater.

B) Column B is greater.

C) Columns A and B are equal.

D) The relationship cannot be determined with the information given.

23.

Column A	Column B
$2715 \div 3$	903

A) Column A is greater.

B) Column B is greater.

C) Columns A and B are equal.

D) The relationship cannot be determined with the information given.

24.

Column A	Column B
The sum of the angles in an isosceles triangle	The sum of the angles in a scalene triangle

A) Column A is greater.

B) Column B is greater.

C) Columns A and B are equal.

D) The relationship cannot be determined with the information given.

25.

Column A	Column B
The number of odd days in March	The number of even days in March

A) Column A is greater.

B) Column B is greater.

C) Columns A and B are equal.

D) The relationship cannot be determined with the information given.

26.

Column A	Column B
The value of the underlined digit 45.67<u>2</u>8	The value of the underlined digit 45.6<u>2</u>78

A) Column A is greater.

B) Column B is greater.

C) Columns A and B are equal.

D) The relationship cannot be determined with the information given.

27.

Column A	Column B
$\sqrt{144}$	$\dfrac{4^5}{4^3}$

A) Column A is greater.

B) Column B is greater.

C) Columns A and B are equal.

D) The relationship cannot be determined with the information given.

28.

Column A	Column B
$4 + 3 \times 5 - 6$	$(4 + 3) \times 5 - 6$

A) Column A is greater.

B) Column B is greater.

C) Columns A and B are equal.

D) The relationship cannot be determined with the information given.

29.

Column A	Column B
The remainder of $247 \div 8$	The divisor of $127 \div 4$

A) Column A is greater.

B) Column B is greater.

C) Columns A and B are equal.

D) The relationship cannot be determined with the information given.

30.

Column A	Column B
The value of b $36 \leq b$	8×2

A) Column A is greater.

B) Column B is greater.

C) Columns A and B are equal.

D) The relationship cannot be determined with the information given.

31.

Column A	Column B
$\frac{1}{4} \times 8$	$\frac{48}{24}$

A) Column A is greater.

B) Column B is greater.

C) Columns A and B are equal.

D) The relationship cannot be determined with the information given.

32.

Column A	Column B
Area of a rectangle with a length of 8 cm and a width of 4 cm	Perimeter of a square with 8 cm sides

A) Column A is greater.

B) Column B is greater.

C) Columns A and B are equal.

D) The relationship cannot be determined with the information given.

33.

Tai has $2.05 in his piggy bank. Juan has $1.98 in his piggy bank.

Column A	Column B
The total number of coins in Juan's piggybank	The total number of coins in Tai's piggybank

A) Column A is greater.

B) Column B is greater.

C) Columns A and B are equal.

D) The relationship cannot be determined with the information given.

34.

Column A	Column B
10 boxes that weigh 4kg each	1 box that weighs 400 grams

A) Column A is greater.

B) Column B is greater.

C) Columns A and B are equal.

D) The relationship cannot be determined with the information given.

35.

Column A	Column B
The number of eggs the baker used per cake if she made 9 cakes and used 3 eggs per cake	The number of miles an athlete runs in a week if they run 4 miles each day for all 7 days

A) Column A is greater.

B) Column B is greater.

C) Columns A and B are equal.

D) The relationship cannot be determined with the information given.

36. A bag of marbles contains 14 red, 30 orange, 2 green, 87 blue.

Column A	Column B
The chance of picking a red marble	The chance of picking an orange marble

A) Column A is greater.

B) Column B is greater.

C) Columns A and B are equal.

D) The relationship cannot be determined with the information given.

37.

Column A	Column B
$\frac{1}{5}$ of $100	Two ten-dollar bills

A) Column A is greater.

B) Column B is greater.

C) Columns A and B are equal.

D) The relationship cannot be determined with the information given.

38.

Column A	Column B
The LCM of 4 and 6	The GCF of 24 and 32

A) Column A is greater.

B) Column B is greater.

C) Columns A and B are equal.

D) The relationship cannot be determined with the information given.

39.

Column A	Column B
$3\frac{2}{8}$	$\frac{13}{4}$

A) Column A is greater.

B) Column B is greater.

C) Columns A and B are equal.

D) The relationship cannot be determined with the information given.

40. Paul swims 50 yards. Treyvon swims 168 feet.

Column A	Column B
The distance Paul swims	The distance Treyvon swims

A) Column A is greater.

B) Column B is greater.

C) Columns A and B are equal.

D) The relationship cannot be determined with the information given.

41.

Column A	Column B
$\left(\sqrt{64}\right) + \left(\sqrt{25}\right)$	The first prime number after 11

A) Column A is greater.

B) Column B is greater.

C) Columns A and B are equal.

D) The relationship cannot be determined with the information given.

42.

Column A				Column B			
The value of x				The value of y			
1	2	3	4	3	4	5	6
12	24	x	48	27	y	45	54

A) Column A is greater.

B) Column B is greater.

C) Columns A and B are equal.

D) The relationship cannot be determined with the information given.

43.

Column A	Column B
$3x + 4 = 16$	$4x + 2 = 18$

A) Column A is greater.

B) Column B is greater.

C) Columns A and B are equal.

D) The relationship cannot be determined with the information given.

44.

Column A	Column B
$\frac{5}{10}$ of 60	$\frac{1}{3}$ of 90

A) Column A is greater.

B) Column B is greater.

C) Columns A and B are equal.

D) The relationship cannot be determined with the information given.

45.

Column A	Column B
The greatest common factor of 27 and 36	The greatest common factor of 32 and 40

A) Column A is greater.

B) Column B is greater.

C) Columns A and B are equal.

D) The relationship cannot be determined with the information given.

46.

Column A					Column B			
The value of x					The value of y			
2	3	4	5		6	7	8	9
$.40	$.60	$.80	x		y	$.70	$.80	$.90

A) Column A is greater.

B) Column B is greater.

C) Columns A and B are equal.

D) The relationship cannot be determined with the information given.

47.

Column A	Column B
$3\dfrac{8}{9} + 6\dfrac{1}{3}$	$11\dfrac{3}{9}$

A) Column A is greater.

B) Column B is greater.

C) Columns A and B are equal.

D) The relationship cannot be determined with the information given.

48.

Column A	Column B
The first prime number after 30.	$5 + 10 \times 3$

A) Column A is greater.

B) Column B is greater.

C) Columns A and B are equal.

D) The relationship cannot be determined with the information given.

49. There are a total of 67 students on the diving and swim teams.

Column A	Column B
The number of students on the diving team	The number of students on the swim team

A) Column A is greater.

B) Column B is greater.

C) Columns A and B are equal.

D) The relationship cannot be determined with the information given.

50.

Column A	Column B
-12	-3×-4

A) Column A is greater.

B) Column B is greater.

C) Columns A and B are equal.

D) The relationship cannot be determined with the information given.

51. Donna's Donuts sells donuts in packs of two and packs of twelve. Which has a higher unit price?

Column A	Column B
A 2 pack for $2.50	A 12 pack for $13.20

A) Column A is greater.

B) Column B is greater.

C) Columns A and B are equal.

D) The relationship cannot be determined with the information given.

52.

Column A	Column B
$\dfrac{6}{2}+\dfrac{10}{5}$	$\dfrac{(6+4)}{2}$

A) Column A is greater.

B) Column B is greater.

C) Columns A and B are equal.

D) The relationship cannot be determined with the information given.

53.

Column A	Column B
The number of hours between 8:30 am and 1:45 pm	330 minutes

A) Column A is greater.

B) Column B is greater.

C) Columns A and B are equal.

D) The relationship cannot be determined with the information given.

54.

Column A	Column B
The value of x if $-8+4x=24$	The value of y if $3y+2y=65$

A) Column A is greater.

B) Column B is greater.

C) Columns A and B are equal.

D) The relationship cannot be determined with the information given.

55.

Column A	Column B
The sum of four right angles	The number of degrees in a circle

A) Column A is greater.

B) Column B is greater.

C) Columns A and B are equal.

D) The relationship cannot be determined with the information given.

Quantitative Test #3 – Answers

1. A	20. C	39. C
2. B	21. B	40. B
3. A	22. C	41. C
4. C	23. A	42. C
5. A	24. C	43. C
6. B	25. A	44. C
7. C	26. B	45. A
8. A	27. B	46. A
9. B	28. B	47. B
10. A	29. A	48. B
11. C	30. A	49. D
12. D	31. C	50. B
13. C	32. C	51. A
14. B	33. D	52. C
15. C	34. A	53. B
16. A	35. B	54. B
17. B	36. B	55. C
18. C	37. C	
19. B	38. A	

Quantitative Test #3 - Explanations

55 Questions – 22 Minutes

---

1. **A**

Column A	Column B
The perimeter of a regular hexagon with sides that are 8 inches long	The perimeter of a pentagon with sides that are 8 inches long
8×6	8×5

2. **B**

Column A	Column B
One interior angle of an equilateral triangle	One interior angle of a rectangle
Smaller than 90 degrees (60 degrees)	90 degrees

3. **A**

Column A	Column B
5^2	$\sqrt{25}$
25	5

4. **C**

Column A	Column B
$8 + 8 + 8 + 8$	$4^2 \times 2$
32	32

5. **A**

Column A	Column B
$\dfrac{3}{4} \times \dfrac{4}{3}$	$\dfrac{4}{16} \times \dfrac{2}{3}$
$\dfrac{3}{4} \times \dfrac{4}{3} = \dfrac{12}{12} = 1$	$\dfrac{4}{16} \times \dfrac{2}{3} = \dfrac{8}{48} - less\ than\ 1$

6. **B**

Column A	Column B
An acute angle	A right angle
Less than 90 degrees	90 degrees

7. **C**

Column A	Column B
$\dfrac{1}{5}$ of 20	$\dfrac{1}{9}$ of 36
$\dfrac{1}{5} \times \dfrac{20}{1} = \dfrac{20}{5} \rightarrow 4$	$\dfrac{1}{9} \times \dfrac{36}{1} = \dfrac{36}{9} \rightarrow 4$

8. **A**

Column A	Column B
The number of factors of 21	The number of factors of 23
1, 21, 3, 7	Prime – just 1 and 23

9. **B**

Column A	Column B
The value of a	The value of a
$2a = 14$	$6 + a = 16$
$2 \times 7 = 14$	$6 + 10 = 16$
7	10

10. **A**

There are 3 boys and 6 girls in group A. There are 2 boys and 11 girls in group B.

Column A	Column B
The ratio of boys to girls in group A	The ratio of boys to girls in group B
$3 : 6$ or $\frac{3}{6}$ or $\frac{1}{2}$	$2:11$ or $\frac{2}{11}$
	Less than $\frac{1}{2}$

11. **C**

Column A	Column B
The smallest factor of 45	The smallest factor of 5
1	1

12. **D**

Column A	Column B
The range of 8 different numbers	The mode of 8 different numbers
No information on the numbers is given, so we cannot know.	

13. **C**

Column A	Column B
The value of x	The value of x
$9x = 72$	$\frac{72}{x} = 9$
$9 \times 8 = 72$	$\frac{72}{8} = 9$
8	8

14. **B**

Column A	Column B
$4^2 + 4^2$	4^4
$4 \times 4 + 4 \times 4$	$4 \times 4 \times 4 \times 4$
$16 + 16$	16×16

15. **C**

Column A	Column B
The pizza with 8 slices	The pizza with 12 slices
Both pizzas are 16-inch pies total. So, they are equal.	Both pizzas are 16-inch pies total. So, they are equal.

16. **A**

Column A	Column B
The mode of: 8, 8, 6, 4, 2, 3, 5	The range of: 8, 8, 6, 4, 2, 3, 5
8 occurs the most times	$8 - 2 = 6$
8	

17. B

A packet of four pencils costs $0.80. Individual pencils cost a quarter.

Column A	Column B
Price of a pencil in the pack	Price of a single pencil
$0.80 \div 4$	0.25
$80 \div 4 = 20 \ SO \ 0.20$	

18. C

Column A	Column B
$30 + 6 + \left(4 \times \dfrac{1}{10}\right)$	Three tens, 6 ones, 4 tenths
$36\dfrac{4}{10}$	$36\dfrac{4}{10}$

19. B

Column A	Column B
$\dfrac{5}{12} \times \dfrac{2}{3}$	$\dfrac{5}{12} \div \dfrac{2}{3}$
$\dfrac{5}{12} \times \dfrac{2}{3} = \dfrac{10}{36}$	$\dfrac{5}{12} \times \dfrac{3}{2} = \dfrac{15}{24}$
Less than half	Over half

20. C

Column A	Column B
$3^2 + 1^{15}$	$3^2 + 1^9$
$9 + 1$	$9 + 1$

21. **B**

Column A	Column B
$10^4 \div 50$	$10^2 \times 200$
$10,000 \div 50$	100×200
$1,000 \div 5$	$20,000$
200	

22. **C**

Column A	Column B
0.42	0.420
	0.42

Adding a 0 after the decimal does not change the value

23. **A**

Column A	Column B
$2715 \div 3$	903
$2700 \div 3 = 900$ $15 \div 3 = 5$	
905	

24. **C**

Column A	Column B
The sum of the angles in an isosceles triangle	The sum of the angles in a scalene triangle
180	180

The sum of the angles in a triangle is always 180 degrees.

25. **A**

Column A	Column B
The number of odd days in March	The number of even days in March

Column A:

30 days
1, 2..... 29, 30
.

If each odd number is paired with an even number, then you will have one odd number left because March always has 31days. Thus there is one more odd day than even days in March.

26. **B**

Column A	Column B
The value of the underlined digit
45.67$\underline{2}$8	The value of the underlined digit
45.6$\underline{2}$78
0.002	0.02

27. **B**

Column A	Column B
$\sqrt{144}$	$\dfrac{4^5}{4^3}$
12	$\dfrac{4 \times 4 \times 4 \times 4 \times 4}{4 \times 4 \times 4}$
	$4 \times 4 = 16$

28. **B**

Column A	Column B

$$4 + 3 \times 5 - 6 \qquad\qquad (4 + 3) \times 5 - 6$$

$$4 + 15 - 6 \qquad\qquad\qquad 7 \times 5 - 6$$
$$19 - 6 \qquad\qquad\qquad\qquad 35 - 6$$

29. **A**

Column A	Column B
The remainder of $247 \div 8$	The divisor of $127 \div 4$
$8 \times 30 = 240$ 7 remaining	4

30. **A**

Column A	Column B
The value of b $36 \le b$	8×2
	16
b is greater than or equal to 36. Any option for b is more than the 16 in column B.	

31. **C**

Column A	Column B
$\dfrac{1}{4} \times 8$	$\dfrac{48}{24}$
$\dfrac{8}{4} = \dfrac{2}{1}$	$\dfrac{2}{1}$

32. **C**

Column A	Column B

Area of a rectangle with a length of 8 cm and a width of 4 cm	Perimeter of a square with 8 cm sides
$8 \times 4 = 32$	$8 \times 4 = 32$

33. **D**

Tai has $2.05 in his piggy bank. Juan has $1.98 in his piggy bank.

Column A	Column B
The total number of coins in Juan's piggybank	The total number of coins in Tai's piggybank
The answer cannot be determined since we do not know if he has mostly quarters or all pennies.	The answer cannot be determined since we do not know if he has mostly quarters or all pennies.

34. **A**

Column A	Column B
10 boxes that weigh 4kg each	1 box that weighs 400 grams
40 kg	1 kg = 1000 g So, less than 1 kg

35. **B**

Column A	Column B
The number of eggs the baker used per cake if she made 9 cakes and used 3 eggs per cake	The number of miles an athlete runs in a week if he runs 4 miles each day for all 7 days
3×9 27	4×7 28

36. **B**

A bag of marbles contains 14 red, 30 orange, 2 green, 87 blue.

Column A	Column B
The chance of picking a red marble	The chance of picking an orange marble
14 reds	30 oranges

37. **C**

Column A	Column B
$\frac{1}{5}$ of $100	Two, ten-dollar bills
$\frac{1}{5} \times 100 = 20$	20

38. **A**

Column A	Column B
The LCM of 4 and 6	The GCF of 24 and 32
12	8

39. **C**

Column A	Column B
$3\frac{2}{8}$	$\frac{13}{4}$
$3\frac{1}{4}$	$3\frac{1}{4}$

40. **B**

Paul swims 50 yards. Treyvon swims 168 feet.

Column A	Column B

The distance Paul swims	The distance Treyvon swims
1 yard = 3 feet 50 yards = 150 feet	168 feet

41. C

Column A	Column B
$(\sqrt{64}) + (\sqrt{25})$	The first prime number after 11
$8 + 5$ 13	13

42. C

Column A	Column B
The value of x	The value of y

1	2	3	4
12	24	x	48

3	4	5	6
27	y	45	54

Column A	Column B
Pattern: Multiply the top number by 12 to get the bottom number. $3 \times 12 = 36$	Pattern: Multiply the top number by 9 to get the bottom number. $4 \times 9 = 36$

43. C

Column A	Column B
$3x + 4 = 16$	$4x + 2 = 18$
$3x = 12$ $x = 4$	$4x = 16$ $x = 4$

44. C

Column A	Column B
$\frac{5}{10}$ of 60	$\frac{1}{3}$ of 90
$\frac{5}{10} = \frac{1}{2}$	$\frac{1}{3} \times 90 \rightarrow \frac{90}{3} = 30$
$\frac{1}{2}$ of 60 = 30	

45. **A**

Column A	Column B
The greatest common factor of 27 and 36	The greatest common factor of 32 and 40
9	8

46. **A**

Column A	Column B
The value of x	The value of y

2	3	4	5
$.40	$.60	$.80	x

Pattern: Add 0.20

$1.00

6	7	8	9
x	$.70	$.80	$.90

Pattern: Add 0.10

$0.60

47. **B**

Column A	Column B
$3\frac{8}{9} + 6\frac{1}{3}$	$11\frac{3}{9}$
$9 + \frac{8}{9} + \frac{1}{3}$	
Will not add to be more than 11	

48. **B**

Column A	Column B
The first prime number after 30	$5 + 10 \times 3$
	$5 + 30$
31	35

49. **D**

There are a total of 67 students on the diving and swim teams.

Column A	Column B
The number of students on the diving team	The number of students on the swim team
The answer cannot be determined. We are not told what fraction are on the diving team or on the swim team.	

50. **B**

Column A	Column B
-12	-3×-4
	12 (A negative times a negative is a positive.)

51. **A**

Donna's Donuts sells donuts in packs of two and packs of twelve. Which has a higher unit price?

Column A	Column B
A 2 pack for $2.50	12 pack for $13.20
$1.25 per donut	$12 \div 12 = \$1$
	$\$1.20 \div 12 = \$0.10$
	$1.10

52. **C**

Column A	Column B
$\dfrac{6}{2}+\dfrac{10}{5}$	$\dfrac{(6+4)}{2}$
$\dfrac{3+2}{5}$	$\dfrac{10}{2}=5$

53. **B**

Column A	Column B
The amount of time between 8:30 am and 1:45 pm	330 minutes
5 hours and 15 minutes	1 hour = 60 minutes 5 hours = 300 minutes 5 hours and 30 minutes

54. **B**

Column A	Column B
The value of x if $-8+4x=24$	The value of y if $3y+2y=65$
$-8+4x=24$ $4x=32$ $x=8$	$5y=65$ *y is larger than 8 (y is 13)*

55. **C**

Column A	Column B
The sum of four right angles	The number of degrees in a circle
$90+90+90+90$ 360	360

SCAT
Scoring

How Scoring Works

Scores

Because the SCAT is a gifted exam, students are compared to those two grade levels above their current grade. Students will receive a percentile score and a scaled score.

When you test matters.

When you test makes a difference! If you are testing in the winter, the cut off score is two points lower if you test before January 1st than if you test after. If you are testing in the summer, it is best to test before June 30th. Before June 30th, you are testing for the grade you just finished. After June 30th, you are testing for the grade you are going into.

Estimating your Scores

The scoring of the SCAT is scaled and can vary based on the test you took.

Five of the questions are experimental and do not count toward the score.

Cut Off Percentages

You can use this chart to *estimate*, but results will vary based on the test.

	Verbal	Quantitative Reasoning
4th Grade – July - Dec	54%	58%
4th Grade – Jan - June	56%	60%
5th Grade – July - Dec	60%	62%
5th Grade – Jan - June	62%	64%

Visit us online!

For more test prep materials, visit us at LarchmontAcademics.com

Made in the USA
Monee, IL
24 September 2024

66483104R00096